The Life Insurance MARATHON

Keep it ***simple*** · Do it ***right***

BY JONATHAN H. MARCROFT

The Life Insurance Marathon

Published by MFS Press

MFS Group, Inc.
3500 South Main Street, Suite 202
South Salt Lake, UT 84115

First Edition
ISBN: 978-1-7349775-0-9 (KDP Black & White Paperback)
ISBN: 978-1-7349775-1-6 (KDP Color Paperback)
Library of Congress Control Number: 2020907768

Editing by Ed Mauss
Cover illustrations by A.D. Whipple
Cover design and graphic consulting by Simon Cooper, WeBrand Digital Marketing
Book design by Mark D'Antoni, eBook DesignWorks

To my extraordinary wife, Lucy Smith Marcroft. You make life a fun and happy adventure! You also read and re-read my writings. And you laugh at my silly jokes. Thank you, Sweetie!

To my incredible mother, Julie Hansen. Your dedication to family, duty and work ethic was etched on my soul as an observant young boy. Thank you, Mom, for being my quiet example. You are my hero!

To my readers: May you find inspiration in this brief poem; encouragement and empowerment in this short book.

EMPOWERMENT

BY JONATHAN H. MARCROFT

When pathways cross, and lives touch,
No matter the space or the time.
You are molded, shaped, readied, primed,
To act in the wake of the clutch.

Stand ready and strong, speak clearly and true.
Waver not from your life's given call.
The molders and shapers, great and small,
Are watching and listening to you.

Be not dissuaded by trials forewarned,
Your well-tested mettle will bear them.
Vigilance, courage and honor through storms,
Will rise above all of the mayhem.

Be mindful of those who regard you with cheer,
Their print has been placed upon you.
The victory is won overcoming your fear,
Of that which you know to be true.

Contents

INTRODUCTION

Who's On Your Side?

Is life insurance on your to-do list?
Does it seem confusing or overwhelming?
Do you have a life insurance policy, but want to shop around?

Before you do anything further, follow your instincts and read this short book. It will simplify everything about life insurance, and put ***you*** in control of this buying decision. You'll be surprised how easy it is when you go into it prepared with some meaningful and relevant knowledge. You'll discover:

- How much you need, and why
- How to budget for this purchase
- Pitfalls to avoid
- How to prepare for the paramedical exam to get the best rate
- How to skip blood and urine testing and still be rated as preferred

- Which type of policy you should buy for **your** situation
- How to find the best policy at the best price
- And much more

The Life Insurance Marathon is not a reference manual. It was written for people just like you who need to know what to do, and why — and also, what ***not to do***, and why. Each successive chapter builds on information from previous chapters, so it is best to read it from start to finish. It will provide you with all of the information and links to tools you need to make a responsible and confident buying decision — a buying decision you won't regret, even many years down the road.

The traditional life insurance sales process is laced with many competing interests. Just like other businesses, life insurance companies have biases toward certain products they offer. Similarly, life insurance agents have their biases about what they want to sell.

"Are you ready for a conflict of interest?"

Lastly, and above all, you want to make an informed decision on life insurance for yourself and your family. And the fact is, ***no one knows your situation better than you.***

Once you have some simple yet strategic knowledge about life insurance, you will know what to look for and what to avoid. You'll know what questions to ask, and you'll have confidence in your own judgement. You won't feel compelled to trust someone else's opinion concerning your family's financial protection.

Let's eliminate your life insurance blind spots! And let's do it in a quick, easy and simple way! No textbooks. No searching opinion articles for hours to find little nuggets here and there. No listening to opinionated — even if well-intentioned — friends or family members about what they think you should do. This book is a simple and straightforward guide to help you think this through and land on what's right for ***YOU***!

Let's get started!!

PART ONE

Develop an Understanding

Simply put, what is life insurance?

How should I plan this expense into my budget?

What if I have group life insurance?

How do I get the best rate for my situation?

CHAPTER ONE

Plan B for Back-Up

What Is Life Insurance, and What *Should It Be for You?*

HAVE YOU EVER TRIED to put your finger on a ball of liquid mercury? Good luck! It will elude you every time. The harder you try, the more frustrating it becomes.

Life insurance can feel like that. The more information you gather, the more confusing it becomes. This chapter will help you understand the simplicity of life insurance as a concept. Once you understand the simple concept, the confusion will melt away, and you'll be in a much stronger position to make a wise product choice.

Many life insurance professionals describe the products they sell in surprisingly optimistic and amicable terms, such as:

- A promise
- An investment
- A supplemental retirement plan
- Your own personal bank
- A gift
- A legacy

There are many other gimmicky descriptions, and frankly, none of them are accurate. This is simply a sales technique used to idealize the product and stimulate the conversation between the insurance professional and you.

Remember this: life insurance is ***a legal contract*** — between you and a huge life insurance company that can easily afford to pay your death benefit. If the contract is ***guaranteed***, and you fulfill your obligation to the contract by making all of your premium payments, then the life insurance company ***must*** fulfill its obligations to you by providing your beneficiaries with all of the guaranteed benefits you purchased. If, on the other hand, the contract is ***non-guaranteed***, then under certain conditions, the life insurance company is ***not required*** to fulfill its original obligations to you, even if you pay every penny you initially agreed to pay. In the insurance industry a contract is called a **policy**.

Now that you understand what life insurance is, let's uncover what it should be for ***you***.

Your Plan B

Life insurance should be simple. Life insurance is a back-up plan; your plan B. It's true that it protects your loved ones, but that's what it does, not what it is. Life insurance will provide your family with financial stability ***if*** an insured loved one dies. So, since its ability as an effective tool relies upon an outcome that is not yet known, it acts as a back-up plan. If you think of life insurance as your family's financial back-up plan, in case of death, you're well on your way to an informed decision.

Principles of Protection

When it comes to choosing a protection plan, there are three guiding principles you should always consider before making a purchase. Whether it is life insurance, I.T. architecture, or a home alarm system, these three principals will help you find the best products and the best design every time.

1. **Security** – Does the plan provide strong guarantees? Is there built-in redundancy? In other words, if something goes wrong, is there

something else in place to prevent losses, so your protection continues unabated? Your protection plan should never be jeopardized by any single point of failure.

2. **Options** – As your situation changes, is your plan scalable to meet your growing or shrinking needs? No one wants to start all over again; it's expensive and time consuming. Design it right the first time, if possible.

3. **Performance** – Will your plan help to meet your goals? Is it cost-effective? Does it require regular oversight, or does it manage itself? If a protection plan requires too many resources and too much management, it becomes counterproductive. If it is cost-effective now, but cost-prohibitive in the future, it becomes unsustainable. Find a healthy balance between simple quality, available resources and long-term sustainability.

These guiding principles will help you to focus and choose a plan that will serve you today, and far into the future.

THE BOTTOM LINE

A life insurance policy is a legal contract between you and a large corporation with very deep pockets. Place yourself in the best position possible by purchasing products with strong guarantees.

- Keep it simple. Purchase products that are either easy to manage, or manage themselves.

- Measure any life insurance purchase with the three guiding principles of protection: security, options and performance.

What's Next

Over the years I have advised many clients with diverse backgrounds, and I have noticed three common threads we all share when considering a life insurance purchase.

1. All of us have both temporary ***and*** lifelong financial protection needs.
2. Everyone wants to get the most out of a life insurance purchase.
3. No one wants to revisit this decision-making process ever again.

The life insurance design you choose — your financial back-up plan — will ultimately determine how these three common threads play out in your planning. There is, however, ***one thing*** that completely dictates your choices. Continue on for this reality check.

CHAPTER TWO

It's a Budget Thing

Are You Committed?

IN MY 20+ YEARS as a licensed life insurance agent, I have worked with countless parents, couples, singles, retirees and business owners from all walks of life, and in just about every life situation imaginable. In every case, there is one factor that completely controls the final decision for a life insurance purchase: affordability. If you can't afford it, nothing else really matters.

I learned early on in my career that people generally buy what they want, as long as it's within their comfort zone. With life insurance, the comfort zone includes more than just available money. It's also about a firm understanding of the product. When we perceive a need, but we aren't confident in our understanding of the product which fulfills that need, we will usually gravitate to the least expensive version of that product; doing so will give us the perception of satisfying our need. Sometimes that approach works out, but usually it doesn't.

Needs vs Wants

There's a lot of competition for our hard-earned money. We are constantly bombarded and distracted by things that cost money — mostly things we don't need. Oftentimes, these are things that look fun and inviting, but in the end, they

don't deliver when it comes to improving our lives. And it takes a lot of discipline to always choose our needs over our wants when we don't have enough money to buy both.

For many people, this tug of war eventually creates enough stress to compel decisions in favor of the wants, which can result in significant risk to ourselves and our family as the needs are delayed. This may sound dramatic, but it is true in nearly everyone's life, especially during our financially vulnerable periods. And in the case of life insurance, being ill-prepared can be devastating.

Emotions vs Logic

In nearly every sales training I have attended during my life insurance career, the presenter inevitably steers the attendees toward an emotional sales presentation. The presenter will say something like, "People buy off of their emotions, so stay away from a logical presentation, as it will only confuse your client and delay a decision." The emotions that respond to a life insurance sales presentation may surprise you, and it is discussed in more detail in a later chapter, *Beware the Gambler*. Emotions certainly play a role when considering a life insurance purchase; however, logic should always direct your purchasing decision.

When you moved into your home, was it emotion or logic that compelled you to set up an account for electricity, gas, and other utilities? It probably wasn't even a thought for you. It's a need, and therefore you didn't even hesitate to bring light, air conditioning, water, refrigeration and cooking into your home. No one needs to explain that utilities are needed to create a healthy home environment.

Life insurance occupies a similar category of need. No one needs to explain that your dependents would be emotionally and financially devastated if you die. Any responsible adult knows this.

A Personal Story – My First Life Insurance Policy

I was 27 years old when I purchased my first life insurance policy. I'm ashamed to admit that life insurance wasn't even a thought for me, though I was married and had two young children with another one on the way. As a sole-proprietor small business owner, group life insurance wasn't an option for me. My family had no financial back-up plan if I died — zero.

Unfortunately, there was no one in my life who took the time to offer me any financial guidance, nor did I seek financial guidance from others. My friend, Eugene, had been newly licensed as a life insurance agent and I bought my first policy from him. It was a term life policy — the only type of policy he sold. I was grateful he brought the need to my attention, but looking back, I wish I'd had a better understanding of the other types of available life insurance policies.

What's Your Budget?

There are numerous variables that control the price of a life insurance policy. However, when it comes to the product itself, your answers to just two questions will control your purchasing decision as it relates to your budget:

1. How much protection do you need?
2. Which type of policy should you purchase to deliver the benefits and outcome you desire?

It's that simple! You don't need to go to a life insurance agent's office to learn what's best for you. You've got this! Start by asking yourself how much you can spend on life insurance — most importantly, your monthly payment range. Can you afford up to $30 per month? Or up to $1,300 per month? Regardless of the amount, it doesn't mean you must spend all of it on life insurance. It just means you ***could*** spend that much without infringing on your other needs.

Lowest Price vs Money Back – What's Your Consumer Style?

Next, ask yourself if you are the type of person who wants your money back if you outlive your protection need, or you just want to pay the lowest price possible. If you want to pay the lowest price, then you need term life insurance. If you want your money back in the likely event you outlive your protection need, then you need guaranteed cash-value life insurance. If you're like me, you buy both types of policies, because they both have value, ***and*** you can still get ***all*** of your money back.

This isn't hard to do. You just need to know how much money is available in your budget for this purchase. And then you need to understand ***and respect*** your buying habits — your consumer style. Once you know that, the rest will quickly come together.

Step 1: Decide how much money you can commit to this purchase on a monthly or annual basis.

Step 2: Understand and respect how you spend money — your consumer style; for example, do you prefer higher quality or lower price?

THE BOTTOM LINE

1. Evaluate how much money you ***can*** spend if you ***needed*** to spend it on this purchase.

2. Determine if you are the type of person who buys the cheapest available products, or whether you will pay more ***if*** there is additional benefit to you that justifies more money.

3. The process of choosing a policy is simple once you know how much you can afford, and you understand your consumer style.

COOL TOOLS

1. Try this easy-to-use Life Insurance Calculator to determine how much protection is appropriate for your circumstances. https://www.simplislife.com/calculator

2. Fill out this short questionnaire, **Policy***Quest,*℠ for a recommendation on the type of policy that would be a good fit for you. https://www.simplislife.com/policy-quest-intro/

3. Use this simple and unique Get a Quote tool to see how much you may need to pay for a term life insurance policy. https://www.simplislife.com/quoter/

What's Next

One of humanity's greatest self-imposed obstacles is false perception. We tend to develop a perception that a product is going to take care of our needs, when in reality, it doesn't measure up to our expectations. And we may not ask a lot of questions, because sometimes we don't know what to ask. Continue to the next chapter to learn about one of the most common false perceptions many people have about their life insurance protection.

CHAPTER THREE

Group Think: The Trap Door

The Story of Group Life Insurance

IN LIFE, WE ARE always navigating trap doors — things that appear to be solid and reliable, but in the end they don't hold up, resulting in an unfortunate consequence. Group life insurance is one of these trap doors, providing a false sense of security.

With group life insurance, you are a certificate holder and your employer is the policy owner. You have no rights to negotiate or change the policy, and you are subject to the policy limits and restrictions. These limits and restrictions are

"Today's meeting is about Getting Beyond Group Think."

unique, and they are rarely explained to you. It is very typical for an employee to simply sign a couple of forms, and bingo, you're on the group life plan. Most employees never meet the selling agent, and never have an opportunity to ask questions to a licensed life insurance professional associated with the employer's group policy.

How It Works

When an employer offers a group life plan, a small amount of protection is provided at no cost to the employee. In addition, there are no health questions or exams. In other words, your acceptance is guaranteed for this small amount of free coverage. Guaranteed acceptance means that the coverage is expensive to the employer, because the life insurance company does not have the opportunity to ask questions about the health of any of the individual employees. Essentially, the life insurance company is going into the contract blind, so they must charge higher prices for the additional risk.

Some group life plans offer additional coverage options to employees. The additional coverage requires some underwriting through an application process, and in some cases a paramedical exam. Oftentimes the employee is responsible to pay the premium related to this additional coverage. Most group life policies increase the premium every five years, and even the additional coverage options tend to outpace the premium expense of individual policies, especially as we enter our 40s and 50s.

Unreliable Benefit

Employers can pull the group life policy rug out from under their employees and retirees with little or no consequence to the company. After Sears declared bankruptcy in 2018, it did just that — ending the group life insurance coverage for 90,000 retirees in March 2019.[1]

Additionally, group life for employees only pays a death benefit if you die while employed with the employer who provides the policy. But very few people die while employed. Generally speaking, people die slowly, over months or years. So, if you're in an accident and you die immediately, or soon after, your group life will pay out. But if you're diagnosed with cancer and you survive for months or years, it's very likely you will not have the group life coverage when you die. Most terminally ill patients end their relationship with their employer because they don't have the energy or stamina to work.

"ER, NO THANKS, SIR... I PREFER TO STAND."

Conversion Impediments

Upon separation from your employment, you may be offered an opportunity to convert your group life insurance certificate into a personally owned cash-value life insurance policy, not to exceed your group life coverage amount. Sears offered retirees this option when it ended their group policy. Conversion to a cash-value policy excludes any underwriting, so your health will not affect your eligibility. However, it will be expensive, especially considering you just lost your income.

You will not qualify for a new, fully underwritten life insurance policy if you have a terminal illness or suffered a terrible accident. If you apply for your own policy at this point, the life insurance company will quickly discover you are not insurable and will deny your application. Remember, the vast majority of people who die during their working years are not employed at the time of death. This is devastating for families who find themselves in this situation.

Be Prepared

Generally speaking, if you become disabled due to accident or illness and you are not able to work, your group life certificate can be extended up to one year ***after your disability begins,*** but ***NOT*** **one year after separation of service** from your employer. That's an important distinction. For example, if you're diagnosed with heart disease and continue to work for six months, but then resign from your employment so you can better manage your stress, your group life insurance will only continue for an additional six months in most cases; because the one year extension of coverage begins from the date you were first diagnosed. After that, you are on your own.

If you are relying on group life insurance, in whole or in part for your family's protection, you are standing on a trap door. Step off the trap door and onto your own life insurance policy that you control, whether or not you are employed. Purchasing your own life insurance policy — before a serious accident or health event occurs — is the most dependable way to financially protect your loved ones against life's uncertainties.

THE BOTTOM LINE

1. Group life insurance is not an effective way to protect your loved ones. But if your employer offers it as a freebie, you should sign up and, at best, consider it a possible supplement to your own life insurance plan.

2. If you suffer a terrible accident or become terminally ill and end your relationship with your employer, your group life coverage may extend for one year after you were diagnosed. After that, you are on your own.

What's Next

To purchase your own life insurance policy, you must go through an underwriting process approved by the life insurance company you choose. The company will look at your age, health, habits and activities that impact your health, and other criteria to determine your rate.

How do you prepare for the underwriting process to secure the best rate for your situation? How do you skip blood and urine testing and still obtain a preferred rate? That and more — in the next chapter.

Under the Microscope

How Is My Rate Determined?

FROM A LIFE INSURANCE company's perspective, ***everything*** about life insurance is risk-based. You represent a risk to the life insurance company when you apply for a policy. If you die while the policy is in-force, the life insurance company will pay your beneficiary the death benefit. Since the death benefit is a substantial amount of money, compared to the premium collected from you, the life insurance company has a strong incentive to reduce their risk through a process called underwriting. After your application is submitted, the underwriting process helps the life insurance company decide if you are a good risk, an average risk, a below average risk, or if they need to decline your application. In other words, they ***really*** want to get to know you.

Have You Ever Applied for a Loan?

It's similar to a loan application process at your bank; you represent a risk to the bank. The bank needs to do their best to determine how likely it is that you will fully pay back the money you borrow. They look at your income, your credit history, years of employment, the collateral you're offering, and more. Then they either deny your loan application, or they offer you the best terms they can based upon the information they have gathered.

The very best loan terms a bank can offer always go to the applicants who don't need the loan. The credit and employment history of these applicants is so stellar, they could easily secure the friendliest terms from another bank because the risk of default is so low. It's a similar process with life insurance, the best rates go to those who are the lowest risk for the life insurance company. The younger and healthier you are, the lower your life insurance premium will be. The opposite is also true. As you age and/or your health declines, your life insurance premium for a new policy will increase.

Here's the great news! Once you lock in a price for a life insurance policy, the price will remain the same ***if*** the policy offers a guaranteed level premium. Even as you age, or your health declines, your premium will still remain the same.[2] Again, this is similar to a loan from your bank. Once you're approved and the loan is funded, your fixed interest rate will not increase due to your changing situation, even if you lose your job and your credit is negatively affected. Similar to a loan from your bank, the life insurance company cannot change the terms in the future.

Getting to Know You

So how does life insurance underwriting work? And what can you do to secure the best rate for your situation? There are five general categories of information that impact your eligibility and rate:

- Age
- Gender
- Health
- Lifestyle
- Financial situation

Every life insurance company is interested in gathering information related to these five categories when underwriting an application for life insurance. While every company gathers similar information, they often have different ways of processing and interpreting the information. For example, some companies specialize in understanding diabetes so they can offer a more accurate rate to diabetics. Others are more general in their understanding of diabetes, and therefore may be less friendly to a diabetic applicant.

If you have a health condition, knowing which life insurance companies offer specialized underwriting for that condition is vital to securing the best rate. The key is to work with a well-organized life insurance agency that has access to many different life insurance companies, and who understands each of their underwriting niches.

HIGH-RISK APPLICANTS CAN STILL GET DECENT RATES

A friend recently approached me to shop a life insurance policy for him. I must admit, I was a bit skeptical about his ability to qualify. He had a stroke four years earlier at the age of 39, but was otherwise in very good health. I submitted a trial application for him to find out if any companies would consider a formal application. Most of the companies declined to cover him or proposed an extreme rate increase for what they call a sub-standard applicant. I was, however, pleasantly surprised to learn that two of the companies were willing to offer a standard rate, pending additional underwriting. Both companies are among the largest in the industry so I felt great about these initial offers.

Like any other industry, life insurance companies have their niches, so don't count yourself out if you have a non-terminal health condition. In most cases there is a company that will offer you a policy, and its rate offer may be a pleasant surprise. Now let's take a closer look at the five categories that determine your rate, and some tips to help you secure the best rate possible.

Age

There are a couple of life insurance concepts related to age that will help you understand how you may capture a better rate.

1. Age has a progressive impact on how much you pay for life insurance. As we age, mortality risk, or the risk of death, increases. Securing a long-term life insurance plan as young as possible is by far the best

strategy to obtain the best rate.[3] You will never be younger than you are today. Waiting only invites the increased possibility that your health will negatively influence your life insurance rate; as we age, we generally develop health conditions. Whether you're in your 20s, 30s, 40s, 50s, 60s, or older, life insurance won't get any cheaper by waiting.

2. Life insurance companies grade on a curve. If you are 55 years old, your health will not be compared to that of an average 25-year-old, but rather to the health of an average 55-year-old. Your rate — whether preferred, standard or sub-standard — will be developed from that grading scale. So, if you're in great health for a 55-year-old, a preferred rate is a strong possibility.

PREFERRED RATES FOR HEALTHY RETIREES

In 2007 I met with a 72-year-old single woman who was struggling to make her mortgage payment. She was on a fixed retirement income, and her only asset was the equity in her home. She needed to find a way to keep her home and she also wanted to leave an inheritance to her children. The last thing she wanted to do was ask her children for financial assistance.

She heard about the reverse mortgage program and contacted a loan officer from a large mortgage lender. The loan officer met with her and made a proposal. She reviewed the information and then contacted me.

When we met, she wanted to find out if it would be less expensive on her fixed income to pay for a life insurance policy that would essentially replace the equity in her home, making her children the beneficiaries of her life insurance as an inheritance to them. Her mortgage payment would be eliminated and she would receive a cash payout of any remaining equity to use as she would like.

I reviewed the details of the reverse mortgage offer and spoke with the loan officer who made the proposal. After careful review, I determined the plan fit her situation. She didn't have any health problems and she was in good shape for her age. I submitted her life insurance application, and after the underwriting was completed the life insurance company offered its best rate: "super preferred." Her life insurance premium would be half the cost of her mortgage payment!

She accepted the offers for both the reverse mortgage and the life insurance policy. I still review her situation annually. Her life insurance policy now has a large cash value with a growing death benefit, and she is still living happily in her home, free of a mortgage payment since 2007.

She recently told me that if she had decided against the reverse mortgage, she would have lost her home during the financial crisis of 2008, when home prices in her area dropped by 50 percent. To this day, she is very grateful to know that her children will benefit from an inheritance through her life insurance policy, regardless of what is happening in the housing market at the time of her death.

Gender

Gender has a low impact on how much you pay for life insurance. On average, women live a few years longer than men. Also, on average, men tend to be more prone to participate in dangerous activities and occupations. So, everything else being equal, women pay slightly less than men for life insurance. This won't help you get a better rate, but it may help you to understand why your gender has an influence on the amount you pay.

Health

Your health plays a vital and significant role in developing your rate for a life insurance policy. Most of the questions in a life insurance application revolve around health. The entire paramedical exam, if required, focuses on your health. And it cannot be overstated that your health status is one of the greatest variables in your life; it can change in an instant.

With
Little Joys
Come Big
Decisions

PARAMEDICAL EXAMS CAN BE REVEALING

Early on in my career, I submitted a life insurance application for a client in his mid-20s. He was married, had a baby, and just started a new business that he financed with credit cards. He didn't have a lot of money for a life insurance purchase, but he felt the responsibility as a parent and a spouse to have some coverage to protect his young family. He appeared to be in great health, so I was confident he would qualify for a preferred rate that would fit his budget.

I was shocked when the offer from the life insurance company came in as a severe sub-standard rating at five times more than the original quote. After I received confirmation from the underwriter that the offer was accurate, I immediately took the offer to my client. I urged him to accept the policy and then immediately see his doctor for a full physical exam; there were some abnormalities in his white blood cell count. He was not happy with the offer and was certain there must have been an error in his blood test results. He couldn't afford the premium, but he had a family to protect, so he followed the first half of my advice and accepted the policy with the intent of shopping around to find a better rate.

Two weeks later he was rushed to the hospital for emergency surgery; his appendix ruptured. The rupture was so severe the surgeon had to conduct exploratory surgery to remove all of the remnants that were now fused to his intestines in order to prevent infection. My client was in the ICU for some time and it was touch-and-go for a while.

When I stopped by the hospital to visit, he expressed his gratitude for my insistence that he accept the policy. He told me the life insurance policy was the one thing that gave him comfort during the time when he thought he might not make it. Needless to say, he kept the policy.

Life insurance companies look at everything related to your health. In addition to the traditional paramedical exam, which includes extensive blood and urine testing, they will pull your Medical Information Bureau (MIB) report and your prescription history report. They may even request an attending physician's statement from your doctor if there is a reason to do so.

Height and Weight

Your build also plays an important role in developing your life insurance rate. Every life insurance company has its own build chart, and every one of them is slightly different. The common thread between all of them is that they are more generous on build than anyone would guess.

Most people who think they're overweight are actually in the preferred build range for life insurance. It's when a person is obese that rates begin to change significantly. Delaying an application for life insurance while dieting and exercising to lose weight is a very common mistake. This strategy doesn't work. Life insurance companies require your weight to be reasonably steady for one year ***after*** losing the weight.

If you truly are overweight, you should secure some life insurance right away, since you are at greater risk for health problems. If weight negatively influences your rate, you can re-submit to future underwriting after you lose some weight; if you keep it off for at least a year, you can secure a better rate. In the meantime, you're covered.

Lifestyle

Lifestyle questions explore the choices you make, both past and present, that positively and negatively impact the risk you represent to a life insurance company. This category may have a significant impact, a low impact, or no impact at all depending on the activity and how it could affect your longevity. Lifestyle questions focus on things such as:

- Nicotine use
- Exercise regimen
- Dangerous activities or hobbies
- Recreational drug use
- Driving record

Nicotine use

Nicotine may have a significant impact on your rate. It is typically categorized by type of product: cigarettes, cigars, pipe, chewing tobacco, vape, hookah, and nicotine gum or patch. Many life insurance companies also include marijuana in this category and rate its use as cigarettes.

Some companies allow a non-tobacco rate if you don't smoke cigarettes. So, if you use other types of nicotine products, but you don't smoke cigarettes, some companies can rate you as a non-tobacco user. If you quit nicotine use, most companies will allow a non-tobacco rate after a certain amount of time has elapsed, typically between one year and three years.

Keep in mind, every company looks at nicotine use in its own unique way.

SHOPPING CAN BE REWARDING

A few years ago, my brother — an avid tobacco chewer — approached me about shopping a life insurance policy for him. He had been paying tobacco rates for almost 10 years and his term life policy was coming to an end. He had gathered quotes from his local agent and learned that his premium was going to triple — and that was a best-case scenario. He considered reducing his life insurance coverage to make the premium more affordable. That's when he reached out to me for some advice.

At the time, I was not yet licensed in the state where he was living. I was sure he would qualify for a non-tobacco rate with a couple of companies, so I secured a life insurance license for his state and submitted his application. The offer came back as preferred non-tobacco. He was blown away that his new 10-year term premium was about the same as his previous 10-year term premium for the same amount of coverage, even though he was now 10 years older!

This type of outcome occurs frequently when there is a specific personal situation for the applicant that fits a niche underwriting criterion for a life insurance company. In this case, a tobacco chewer who doesn't smoke cigarettes qualified for a non-tobacco rate with a very well-known life insurance company.

Exercise regimen

Some companies have started giving credit to applicants who exercise regularly. This generally has a low impact on your rate, but the credit can be progressive as you stick with your exercise regimen, so your premium can actually decrease over time. One company has an app that helps you stay on track. Pretty cool!

Hazardous activities or hobbies

The impact of this category varies widely depending on the activity, and your level of participation. These activities include, but are not limited to: piloting non-commercial aircraft, rock climbing, scuba diving, race car driving, rodeo competition, and skydiving. Many life insurance companies will decline coverage for an applicant who participates in these activities, unless the applicant agrees to an exclusion of coverage if death occurs from a related accident. This is the most common outcome. In some cases, however, an exclusion of coverage may not be required, depending on the activity and your level of participation.

If you secured a life insurance policy prior to participation in a hazardous activity, that policy may cover a claim that occurs as a result of participation in that activity. Life insurance companies may not deny a claim that results from an activity you were not engaged in prior to your application date.

Recreational drugs

In years past, recreational drug use has been a big red flag for life insurance companies, usually resulting in a denial of coverage. In more recent years, with the legalization of marijuana increasing on a state-by-state basis, underwriting procedures and decisions are beginning to soften toward cannabis.

Most companies will differentiate recreational use from prescription use. Most will also treat marijuana as nicotine use for rating purposes, although some companies will provide a non-tobacco rating for marijuana consumers. As laws and regulations continue to change toward legalizing marijuana use, life insurance companies will likely respond in kind.

Other types of recreational drug use will often result in a denial of life insurance coverage.

Driving record

Most of us don't think about how our driving record might influence our life insurance rates. Driving is one of the most hazardous activities we do on a daily basis. Your driving record could have a significant impact on your rate if you have a lot of moving violations on your record, or numerous accidents.

THE SPEEDING BRIDE

Marriage is a life event that often motivates people to seek out some life insurance. One of my clients referred their oldest son to me when he and his fiancée were married. It turns out his new bride was a young woman I worked with on the paramedical exam side of the business. I always requested her services for my clients since she was prompt, thorough and friendly. She did a great job!

They both applied for a life insurance policy. His application flew right through the process at a preferred rate. Hers was a different story. She had 13 speeding tickets on her driving record. Ouch!! The life insurance company was willing to offer a policy, but only at sub-standard rates.

Though I strongly encouraged her to accept the coverage offer and resubmit to underwriting for a better rate in a year, she decided to delay until her driving record improved. A year later, eight of her speeding tickets had fallen off her driving record. I submitted a new application for her, and this time the life insurance company offered her a standard rate.

When your job requires a lot of driving hours, you may rack up moving violations. Life insurance companies seriously consider your driving record before they issue a policy.

Financial situation

Your financial situation can affect your eligibility for a life insurance policy. Many companies will not issue a policy on someone who is in an active bankruptcy. This is generally the only financial situation that impacts eligibility on a life insurance application.

As a side note, if a cash-value life insurance policy is secured prior to a bankruptcy, the cash value may be protected from the bankruptcy court.[4]

Look Your Best: Paramedical Exam Tips

The paramedical exam is a vital part of the traditional, full underwriting process. This is when your rate is generally determined. It's very important that you are prepared to present your best possible self. Think of this as your first date with someone you really like; you want to look your best!

Here are a few tips to help you prepare and obtain the best results:

DO:

- Get a good night's sleep.
- Drink a tall glass of water about two hours before your exam.
- Try to make your appointment time within an hour or two of waking after six to eight hours of sleep, and don't eat prior to the exam. If this is not possible, avoid eating for at least two hours prior to your exam time.

- Choose a calm, relaxing setting for the location of your exam — most people are more relaxed at home, and more stressed at work; wherever your blood pressure will be lower, make that your exam location.
- Eat a healthy salad for dinner the night before your exam, or at least two hours prior to your exam; but skip anything with high cholesterol, such as shrimp and granola.
- Keep your shoes on, with heels up to one inch (such as tennis shoes), while measuring your height; remove shoes and empty pockets before stepping on the scale.
- Wear comfortable, loose-fitting clothes; stay away from heavy clothing, as this will affect your weight on the scale.

DON'T:

- *Don't* drink alcoholic beverages for at least 12 hours prior to your exam, or a lot of alcohol the night before.
- *Don't* smoke for at least two hours prior to your exam.
- *Don't* drink caffeinated beverages for at least two hours prior to your exam.
- *Don't* exercise or engage in other strenuous physical activity for 24 hours prior to your exam; this can cause trace amounts of blood to enter your urinary tract.

On the day of your exam, if you feel out of sorts or you forget to prepare, do not hesitate to reschedule. You only have one chance to make a good first impression. This is especially true for a life insurance paramedical exam.

Accelerated Underwriting: Still Great Rates – No Exam

In recent years, some life insurance companies have started to offer a more friendly process called accelerated underwriting. This allows you to obtain an accurate rate ***without the paramedical exam, or blood and urine testing***. That means no needles, no urine sample, no height and weight measurement, and no blood pressure reading.

In today's digital world, life insurance companies can obtain access to most of the information they need to rate an applicant accurately without invading anyone's personal space. Accelerated underwriting is a valuable tool for life insurance companies because it reduces underwriting costs. This is a growing trend within the life insurance industry and is increasing in popularity with the general public.

There are a few things you need to understand about this program:

- Not all companies offer it, but many do — and the number is growing.
- Not everyone qualifies; every company has its own set of rules for age and coverage restrictions.
- Even if you are a good fit for accelerated underwriting, most companies give themselves the right to pull an application out of that process and require full underwriting.
- If you choose accelerated underwriting for your application, the policy will likely be issued much faster, typically between one day and three weeks, compared to six to eight weeks for traditional, full underwriting.
- Companies that offer accelerated underwriting often issue policies at preferred rates under this program. Whatever your risk classification would be using full underwriting, you're likely to receive the same risk classification using accelerated underwriting.

THE BOTTOM LINE

We've covered a lot of important information in this chapter that will help you secure the best rate possible for your situation. Nevertheless, I always have mixed feelings about discussing this information. I have seen people misinterpret the key message as, "if you just wait a few more months while you prepare, you can get a better rate." To that, I say ***NO, NO and NO!!*** That is ***not*** the message! ***Never*** delay your application for life insurance. After securing coverage, you can always re-submit your application at a later date to obtain a better rate if you are not ecstatic about your original rate.

What's Next

Life after death can be a provocative topic, and oftentimes leads to interesting conversations. In the world of life insurance, life after death is not about those who've died, it's about the loved ones left behind — those who now are picking up the pieces and continuing on with ***their*** life after ***your*** death.

Death causes emotional trauma, and it can sometimes cause financial struggle, or even devastation. How much life insurance protection would your loved ones need to leave them in a stable financial position, so they can focus on the emotional healing side of this experience rather than scrambling to pay the bills? The next chapter reveals this and more.

INTERMISSION

Author's Q&A

What interest does the author have in writing this book?

I am a licensed life insurance agent, and the president of a multi-state life insurance agency corporation, MFS Group, Inc., that works with many different life insurance companies. MFS Group, Inc. is the parent corporation of Simplis® Life, which specializes in educating the public about life insurance topics, and selling life insurance policies through a secure website and over the phone.

Simplis Life was founded on the principle of ***consumer empowerment***. Comprehensive, yet simple-to-use tools are available to anyone who visits us at www.simplislife.com. My business goal is to educate the public about responsible and common-sense life insurance planning, and to sell well-designed, high-quality and budget-friendly life insurance policies to people in all stages of life. My personal goal is to influence ***positive change for consumers*** within the life insurance industry. Consumer empowerment is the most effective approach to create such a change.

At Simplis® Life, our motto is Best Policy / Best Price. We shop many different life insurance companies to find the highest quality policy at an affordable price for you. We then design a plan that will deliver the best outcome. This means placing you in a policy with strong guarantees, some of which allow you to recoup all of your premium expenses. If you decide to cancel your policy in the future, you can receive all of your money back with the right plan.

I take full responsibility and stand behind all of my opinions expressed in this book. My opinions about life insurance have evolved over decades as I have seen the various results, both positive and negative, from working with countless clients, and from my own personal experience of owning life insurance. My opinions are based solely upon my professional observations of real-life situations and outcomes, and my own personal experience.

Where are the charts and graphs in this book?

The Life Insurance Marathon does not contain any charts or graphs, and there is limited technical language used throughout the book. My goal is to help you, not confuse you. I want to answer your questions — not create 10 more in your mind.

When you understand the concepts that control life insurance products, the details that are ***meaningful to you*** take shape quickly. You can then make decisions based upon your preferences, rather than the confusion that ensues from numerous charts and graphs that may or may not be accurate in a future outcome.

What inspired you to write this book?

As mentioned earlier, my personal goal is to influence positive change for consumers within the life insurance industry. It is my hope that this book will help empower consumers to create such a change, by delivering vital and actionable information in a manner that most people can understand and digest.

Every part of this book stems from two questions I asked myself:

1. From my experience as a consumer, what would I want to know if I knew nothing about life insurance and I was in the market to purchase a policy?

2. From my knowledge and experience of how life insurance products actually work, what is most important for consumers to know before making a purchasing decision?

These two questions guided everything from the general topics covered, all the way down to the specifics of how to get the best rate. The real challenge in putting this material together in a consumer-centric way was to make it an interesting read. I hope you find the content simple, helpful and thought-provoking. The last thing I want to write is a boring book!

This is not a comprehensive life insurance textbook, handbook or reference manual. This book is designed for those with a busy lifestyle who need quick, focused and relevant information about life insurance, delivered in an interesting and memorable way. If you need life insurance, and you're not a life insurance professional, this book is for you!

Did you ever make any mistakes with your own life insurance planning?

Yes. When I was still a relatively new life insurance agent, but established well enough to feel financially secure, I decided to purchase two large non-guaranteed life insurance policies — one for myself and one for my spouse. Management for the company I represented at the time, strongly encouraged agents to purchase the products we sold, and I was excited to feel I had finally reached a point where I could participate in stock market returns with my life insurance. Things were going well with my career, and I felt very confident about the future. I was also able to now tell my clients that most of my own coverage was variable life insurance.

My financial commitment to these two policies was more than $1,000 per month. Within a couple of years, the company I represented made some major changes that created substantial sales obstacles, and my new business sales significantly declined. My income was based on commission, and the majority of my commission was earned from new sales. Within months my income declined by more than 50%. Additionally, the stock market was also declining precipitously. It was a perfect storm scenario. Before the stock market recovered, both policies had lapsed. I was not able to keep up with the scheduled premium payments, and the variable cash value within the non-guaranteed policies declined at a rapid rate, in line with stock market performance, or lack thereof. It was extremely frustrating to witness the implosion of a product that was so basic to my own personal planning. I lost a lot of money because I made two mistakes:

1. I was overly confident in my ability to generate an income and therefore I overcommitted to an unsustainable payment. I did not take into account that my income could be negatively affected by decisions made outside my control. That was naïve for a commission based professional.

2. I purchased a long-term financial protection product that is dependent upon stock market performance. When the stock market declined by 50%, the cash value in my policies also declined by 50%. Life insurance fees and money management fees were still being withdrawn from the cash value in my policies, and at the same time, I was not able to pay the premium. It didn't take long for these policies to lapse.

This is not an easy story for me to share, because it's difficult to admit I made this kind of error. But until this happened to me, I didn't truly understand the serious risks involved with non-guaranteed life insurance policies tied to stock market performance, and as a result I learned a valuable lesson.

Soon after this experience, I carefully analyzed all life insurance policy types. This is when I began to develop what is essentially a bullet-proof life insurance plan, I call *The Balancing Act*℠, which is explained at the end of this book.

It is my sincere hope that, after completing this book, you will feel confident and empowered to take action on an informed decision regarding your life insurance coverage that is right for you and your loved ones.

Cheers!

Jon Marcroft

PART TWO

Make Some Decisions

How much protection do I need?

How long do I need protection?

What are the pitfalls to avoid?

What policy types are best for me?

CHAPTER FIVE

Dead Man's Bounty

How Much Do I Really Need?

ONCE UPON A TIME everything in life worked out exactly as planned...NOT! Life has a way of keeping things interesting. There are the curve balls, the speed bumps, the under-the-bus experiences, and other personal growth "tonics" for humility that are ever-present for those of us who need life insurance — the living. We get it! "If I die, someone is going to feel like they just got thrown under the bus!" And that's if you have enough life insurance coverage. If you don't, the feeling of meeting a freight train in a dark tunnel comes to mind. Choo...choo!

As a life insurance agent, one of the toughest questions to answer for a client is, "How much life insurance do ***you*** think I need?". The vocal emphasis on "you" is very telling. It gives the impression of a loaded question, especially when meeting with a married couple. Two different people, whom I now perceive, may have two different ways of prioritizing this decision. While mentally scrambling to identify which one is the "decision maker", an agent might think, "I hope I don't lose one of them as I meander through my response." And so, the dance begins. It's a silly way of approaching such a serious and sometimes difficult subject. But it's the traditional way this has been done for many, many years.

Let's put all of that aside, place you in the driver's seat, and focus on what really matters for your family:

- Freedom,
- Emotional health, and
- A familiar lifestyle.

Once you have a better understanding of these three priorities as they relate to life insurance, you will be able to identify an appropriate range of coverage for your family. Let's dive into the information and tools you need to answer the question, "how much do I really need?"

Social Security and the Freedom Conundrum

Before I founded Simplis® Life, I worked as a captive agent for four different life insurance companies. Not one of them ever trained me on Social Security Survivors' benefits for spouses and dependent children. It was mentioned, but it was never covered in detail, nor was the subject ever discussed in terms of incorporating the information into a presentation. I had to research it and gain this knowledge on my own. Mind boggling! And it's unfortunate. I think most agents don't understand how powerful this knowledge becomes when discussing life insurance needs with parents of minor children.

Did you know that if you have surviving minor dependents when you die, they are eligible for Social Security Survivors' benefits? That's right! If your child is under age 16, the surviving parent or legal guardian will receive the benefit. If your child is between age 16 and 18 (up to age 19 if attending elementary or secondary school full time), your child will receive the benefit directly. Your surviving spouse is also eligible for survivors' benefits at age 60, unless your spouse is disabled, in which case the surviving spouse eligibility age is 50.[5]

"Listen, I understand about the burden of exposition, but can we just get to how much protection we need?"

It's a great program, and the average benefit payment is $885 per survivor each month (your benefit amount may be higher or lower).[6] As with any benefits provided by the government, it comes with strings attached. That's okay, if your family is not dependent upon these benefits. If, however, your surviving family members don't have enough money from another source to support their needs, they will become dependent on these benefits, and important decisions may be strongly influenced by the possibility of losing some or all of them. Additionally, when children turn 16 years old, the benefit is paid directly to them, which can lead to internal family issues if your surviving spouse is dependent upon the benefits to pay the bills. These are important reasons to consider having an appropriate amount of life insurance in addition to leveraging these survivors' benefits.

The survivors' benefits are based upon the decedent's projected Social Security retirement benefit at the time of death. The benefit is reduced when a survivor is working and earns more than $17,640 annually for the year 2019.
This allowable amount of annual earnings increases slightly each year and can have a significant impact on the benefits available if your surviving spouse is career oriented.[6]

While survivors' benefits are reduced if a survivor earns more than the maximum allowable income, a large balance in a bank account has no affect on the benefits. Your surviving spouse could have a million dollars in the bank and would still receive the full benefit amount. This is another example of why it's important to have enough life insurance protection. Your beneficiary receives the death benefit from the life insurance company, and now has access to money that is not controlled by the government. Your career-oriented spouse could continue earning a good living, and yes, the survivors' benefits will be reduced due to your spouse's earnings, but there's a million dollars in the bank, so the reduction in benefits won't impact your family's needs. On the other hand, your spouse may choose to take a leave of absence from work to be a stay-at-home parent. In this scenario, the family will receive the full survivors benefits and have the same million dollars in the bank.

Social Security Survivors' benefits should certainly be taken into account when considering your family's life insurance needs; however, it should be considered a secondary support system. In other words, if they need the benefits, the benefits are there. If they don't need them, the benefits can be saved for future needs, such as higher education costs.

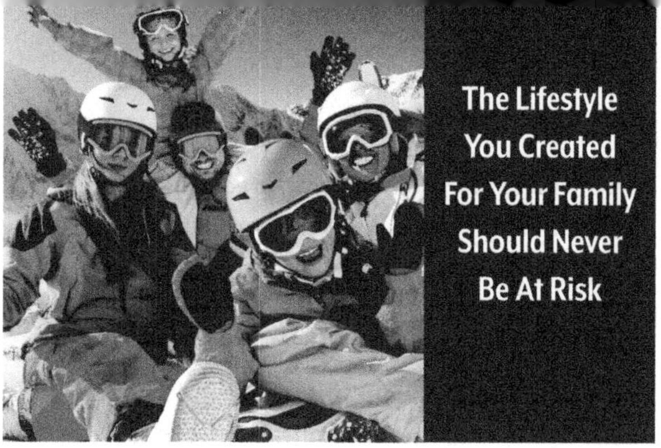

Money can't buy happiness, but it can buy options, and options can help to support a happy and fulfilling life. By leaving your beneficiary more than enough money to continue the lifestyle you helped to create, there is a much higher probability of things continuing down the path you intended. Options also allow your beneficiary to navigate life's curve balls easier and more successfully.

The Emotional Cost of Death

For most people, death is an emotionally charged event. Even when it's expected, we struggle between the peaceful rest of our deceased loved one, and our own sense of loss. Grieving is a natural process of feeling stuck between the need to let go and accept the reality of death, and the desire to express our feelings to our now deceased loved one. In most cases, when the decedent had been very ill over a long period of time, or was elderly, grieving can occur naturally as we go through our normal daily activities. But when death comes at an unexpected time, grieving the loss can be more complicated, and can take much longer.

Most of us don't like to think about death, and few want to talk about an actual plan if it were to happen. Yet death is the one thing we can plan for because we know it's in our future; we just don't know the details. If we plan wisely, we never need to think about it again in terms of making a plan.

In my experience, it is difficult — if not impossible — to emotionally prepare for the loss of a loved one. However, we **can** prepare for the financial impact, and that can help to curb negative emotions, as well as promote supportive emotions. Strong financial preparation provides the breathing room we need to properly grieve the loss of our loved one. Weak financial preparation leads to added stress and pressure, which then leads to fear, anger and further sadness. It's very difficult to focus on healing when you're trying to figure out how to pay the bills and put food on the table. It's also very difficult to create a peaceful space for yourself when you must impose on others because you need their support. Moving back home with mom and dad because you can't afford to stay in your own home can feel humiliating and intrusive, even though your family is eager to help.

Emotion Strings

Emotion strings can help you better understand some of the feelings that family members may experience after the loss of a loved one. The four generalized emotions we feel are: Sadness, Anger, Fear and Happiness.[7] Emotion strings can reveal the more specific underlying emotions which create the generalized emotional response. Since we're reviewing the emotional impact of financial support through life insurance, or the lack thereof, let's focus on emotions which are more likely to develop from this situation, whether positive or negative.

Example: When I feel sad, usually my sadness is a generalized emotional response to a much deeper and more specific emotion. Sad may stem from a feeling of loneliness. And loneliness may stem from a feeling of abandonment. Abandonment may stem from a feeling of isolation. In this example, my true emotion is isolation, which I express by acting like, or saying, "I'm sad".

I invite you to do an exercise. As you review the following emotion strings, think of yourself as the decedent, and then as a survivor. As the decedent, how do you want your loved ones to feel about the financial support you provided to them after your death? As a survivor, how will you feel about the financial support your deceased loved one left for you?

Your family's financial stage has been set, and now the survivors are faced with their transition into a new life.

Emotion String #1

- **Sad** – Abandoned – Victimized (Lack of financial support, when it could have been available, can feel like victimization. For example, as a high school student you are forced to drop out of team sports because of the expenses to participate.)

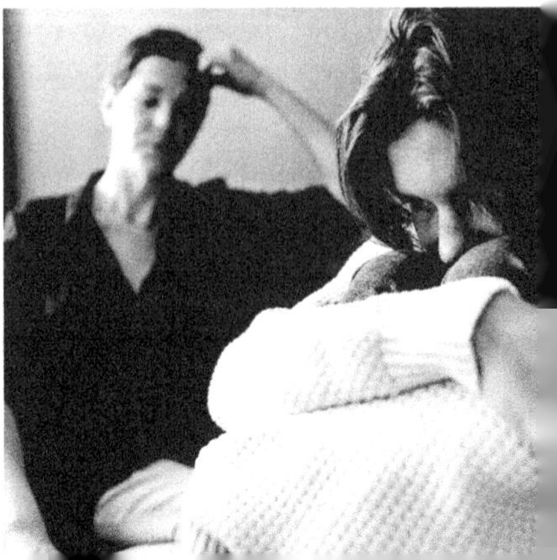

- **Angry** – Resentful – Violated (We become resentful when we feel we have been wronged.)
- **Fearful** – Humiliated – Disrespected (Respect stems from caring for others and having their backs. Disrespect stems from lack of planning to provide for the needs of our loved ones.)
- **Happy** – Proud – Respected – Confident (Your children and spouse know you took care of them. You always had their backs, even in death.)

Emotion String #2

- **Sad** – Desperate – Vulnerable (Lack of financial support can create a feeling of vulnerability.)
- **Angry** – Hurt – Devastated – Embarrassed (Think of the young family asking the community for donations to help cover the cost of a funeral.)
- **Fearful** – Insecure – Inadequate (Lack of financial support can contribute to insecurity.)
- **Happy** – Optimistic – Inspired (There is a lot of time to support each other through the grieving process. Though hearts are broken, your loved ones can feel optimistic about their future.)

Emotion String #3

- **Sad** – Lonely – Abandoned – Isolated (It's easy to feel isolated when you can't afford counseling, or can't take a trip to get away for a while.)
- **Angry** – Frustrated – Irritated (Frustration happens when we don't have the power or finances to change our situation.)
- **Fearful** – Anxious – Overwhelmed – Hopeless (Being forced to work

full time to support your family, while at the same time helping family members through a grieving period can lead to these emotions.)

- **Happy** – Peaceful – Hopeful – Loving (No one is stressed about the bills, so there is plenty of time to grieve and heal. By being properly prepared, you helped to create a loving environment and an attitude of hopefulness for your loved ones.)

I hope you found this exercise to be helpful. It can be difficult to think through the variety of real-life issues you would face as a surviving spouse of dependent children, or any other survivor situation. Going through the grieving process is a cost a family must bear when a loved one dies. These emotions are less tangible than other costs related to death. Nonetheless, the ability to grieve in a healthy way is clearly one of the most important considerations when selecting an appropriate amount of coverage for your family.

Lifestyle Protection and the Repurposing of Your Coverage

The theory of insurance is to make the affected people "financially whole" after a covered loss occurs. In the case of life insurance, that means you should not suffer a ***financial*** loss due to the death of a loved one. Life insurance is somewhat unique in the claim process. Upon death, the claim is very straightforward — the death benefit is paid to the beneficiary.

With auto insurance, when your vehicle is in an accident, the insurance company determines the value of the vehicle. In other words, the auto insurance company is responsible for determining what it means for you to be made financially whole. But with life insurance, that responsibility is yours; you determine the amount of coverage your beneficiary needs to be made financially whole.

When it comes to developing an accurate range of coverage, I subscribe to a lifestyle needs-based approach which includes repurposing the protection as your needs change. Repurposing is discussed in greater detail in an appendix article of this book, entitled, *The Balancing Act*℠.

Your needs are determined in a simple, two-step process:

1. Final expenses: if you live a long life, how much money will your beneficiary need to pay for your final expenses?

2. Lifestyle protection: if you die tomorrow, how much money will your beneficiary need to continue the lifestyle you helped to provide? (Notice we're focused on lifestyle rather than income.)

Final Expenses

Today, the average cost of a funeral and standard burial in the United States is about $10,000.[8] This can vary significantly depending upon the region of the country. You should conduct your own research to determine the average cost for your area. The future cost of a funeral is expected to outpace standard inflation.

Other considerations:

- If you die while traveling, your body will need to be transported; this can be a significant cost.
- There may be some end-of-life healthcare expenses not covered by your medical insurance.
- You may leave some outstanding debt which needs to be paid.

The average cost of cremation with funeral services is roughly $6,500,[8] again depending on your location. The other considerations still apply.

My Advice

Obtain a generous amount of final expenses coverage by purchasing a guaranteed cash-value life insurance policy for the long term. If you're under 40 years old, the policy should be at least $100,000 of coverage. If you're 40 to 55, it should be at least $75,000. If you're over 55, it should be at least $50,000. You'll never be sorry you purchased this coverage, and those who are left to handle your final needs will appreciate, and admire, your preparation and thoughtfulness.

Lifestyle Protection

How much money would it take to support your family's current lifestyle without anyone producing an income for the next 5 to 20 years? Lifestyle protection encompasses everything financial in your life: income, debt, family services, education, vacations, etc. The process to determine an accurate range of coverage is simple.

Step one: ask your beneficiary

This is a very important conversation. As the insured owner of the policy, you will determine your level of life insurance protection for your survivors. Your beneficiary, who will be a surviving loved one if you pass away, deserves to provide input regarding your level of life insurance protection.

If your beneficiary doesn't want to provide input for any reason, don't force the issue; it's not worth the argument. Their talents lie outside the realm of finance. Simply choose a coverage on the higher side of your family's range of need. Your beneficiary will need the extra padding if finance isn't a strength.

Step two: develop your range of need

Choose one of the following three scenarios. Then gather the financial information identified in that scenario.

(These scenarios are designed primarily for a married couple with minor children. If you are a single parent with minor children, these scenarios still apply. Simply replace the words "your spouse" with the name of the person who will raise your child(ren) if you pass away. If you don't have children, or your children are raised, in addition to scenarios #1 and #3, you will want to consider Empty Nesters and Retirees, page 54.)

Scenario #1

If both you and your spouse currently work, and your surviving spouse will continue to work, calculate your coverage needs based upon:

- Your total after-tax annual earnings multiplied by the number of years your family will need the income.

Scenario #2

If you are a stay-at-home parent, and your surviving spouse will continue to work, calculate your coverage needs based upon:

- The average cost of raising a child in the United States, which is approximately $12,980 annually per child in a middle-income ($59,200-$107,400), two-child, married-couple family.[9] Your cost may be higher or lower than the average. Multiply the annual cost by the number of years remaining to raise your child(ren). The right life insurance needs calculator (see page 54) comes in very handy for this calculation.

Scenario #3

If you want your surviving spouse to have the option to be a stay-at-home parent, calculate your coverage needs based upon:

- ***Total*** household after-tax annual earnings multiplied by the number of years your family will need the income.

In all three of these scenarios, you will also need a good understanding of:

- Your total debt, broken down into categories (mortgage, auto loan, credit cards, etc.).
- Higher education funding for your minor children and/or your surviving spouse.

Choose one of the three scenarios that best describes your desire for your surviving loved ones. Use the simple (and free) Life Insurance Calculator created by Simplis Life (see Cool Tool, page 54). It's very easy to use. Simply enter your information to arrive at your coverage amount. You can easily adjust the calculator to find the right amount of coverage for your needs. There are also many different ways to fine-tune the calculator to arrive at your desired coverage amount.

Household earned income supports a family's financial lifestyle. Your debt payment obligations are likely paid from your earnings. If you are generous with your income replacement, you may not need to include any debt payoff in your calculation. It is, however, wise to provide your loved ones with more than adequate life insurance protection in order to help relieve some of the stress that accompanies the grieving process. The ability to pay off the mortgage and still have enough money for income replacement while raising a family, and figuring out the future, will provide some additional stability during a very difficult time.

COOL TOOL

Try this simple, effective and unique life insurance needs calculator. This will help you understand how much life insurance protection your loved ones need.

Life Insurance Calculator
https://www.simplislife.com/calculator/

Empty Nesters and Retirees

The principles employed to develop a range of financial protection apply to anyone who has a need for life insurance. Simply use the Simplis Life Insurance Calculator to arrive at your coverage need. Here are a few additional items to consider:

- Do you want to leave an inheritance to your heirs through life insurance? (Note: life insurance proceeds payable to a living person are not subject to probate.)

- Would you like the option to use part of your life insurance policy death benefit to pay for a future long-term care need while you're still living?

Some life insurance policies offer unique and valuable benefits to retirees and pre-retirees. In many cases, it is easier to qualify for long-term care benefits through a life insurance policy, and you have greater flexibility in using the benefits.

THE BOTTOM LINE

When you take some time to figure out your actual needs, and then create a plan that allows for some flexibility with guarantees, *The Balancing Act*,℠ you will never need to revisit this subject again. As the old saying goes, "measure twice, cut once." Do it right the first time, so you never need to overhaul your life insurance planning in the future. Now, that would be a great happily-ever-after story!

What's Next

When something seems too good to be true, it probably is. Life insurance companies offer many different products, but their favorites are the non-guaranteed types of policies. The next chapter focuses on these policy types, and the reasons why some of them may look good, but in the end might not deliver on their non-guaranteed "promises".

Questions about anything covered in this chapter?
We have answers — info@simplislife.com or (888) 385.1711
www.simplislife.com

CHAPTER SIX

Beware the Gambler and the Allure of Greed Over Need

The Story of the Non-Guaranteed Life Insurance Policy

"HOW DO YOU ***FEEL*** about life insurance?" When I worked as a field agent (meeting potential clients in their homes) I always began my presentation with this simple question. With few exceptions, people paused to search for an answer, as if it never crossed their mind. The answers ranged between, "I feel it's important for my family", to "I think it's a total rip off!" (that guy didn't pause).

Over the years I tracked the responses with great interest. Honestly, this short exchange was, for me, the most interesting part of my presentation. About 80 percent stated they feel that life insurance is like gambling. Think about that: 80 percent! That was a very enlightening nugget of insight for a young field agent.

"You're right," I would reply in an agreeable tone. "With some policies, it is like gambling. But it's the bet you ***don't*** want to win." We would chuckle, maybe tell each other a gambling story or two, and then move into my presentation. I felt that most of these people appreciated the humanity of my approach, and were perhaps a bit surprised, if not intrigued, by the transparency.

Transparency is key to the success of any business in this day and age. And yet, for the average consumer, transparency is hard to find in the life insurance industry. Life insurance companies are highly secretive about how they develop their rate structures. They have also created increasingly complex products over the years in an attempt to compete with other financial products offered by investment brokers in the retirement planning space. This behavior has led to consumer distrust of the life insurance industry as a whole, and rightfully so. Why?

1. As consumers, most of us want simplicity and guarantees from the products we rely upon for our needs.

2. We tend to feel uncomfortable buying a product when we have little or no understanding about how our price point is determined.

3. For most of us, a life insurance policy is not a retirement plan.

In my experience, the three preceding statements are true. Alternatively, in my experience, the following three competing statements are also true:

1. As consumers, most of us are attracted to the potential for higher gains from a sexy "investment grade," non-guaranteed and flexible premium life insurance policy, when compared to the old reliable, slow-to-grow, simple and guaranteed policy.

2. After the "greed" emotion sets in, from the perceived promise of strong gains, who cares how the price point is determined, as long as it's affordable right now.

3. "I can use this for my retirement? And not pay any income taxes? Sign me up!"

"I understand past performance is no guarantee of future results, but I'm a little confused by your winking and air quotes."

Have you ever found yourself looking back and wishing you had purchased a brand-new car, rather than your now, broken-down used car? After the many repairs over the years on your used car, the new car may have cost about the same, and with far fewer interruptions in your life. That said, I would much rather be stuck with a broken-down car than a broken-down life insurance policy.

GREED IN LIFE INSURANCE DECISIONS

Greed, in this context, means the act of prioritizing the potential for financial gain ***over*** the need for guaranteed protection. It is a powerful consumer emotion, triggered by the positive desire to accomplish more with a single purchase. For example, when life insurance can be represented as an investment that could enhance a retirement portfolio, suddenly it becomes worthy of greater attention, and more of your money. Unfortunately, many people have bought into this concept without fully understanding the long-term ramifications of their purchase. Agents are often trained to tap into this powerful consumer emotion, oftentimes presenting the investment as the primary selling point, and life insurance as a "tax friendly" vehicle for the investment.

A life insurance policy becomes weak, unhealthy and broken-down when it is underfunded. This can happen for a variety of reasons, but it boils down to a couple of different scenarios: (1) either you aren't paying your premium, or (2) your non-guaranteed "investment-grade" policy is underperforming and can no longer support the cost of your death benefit (otherwise known as mortality cost).

Mortality cost is always rising in a life insurance policy; there are no exceptions. Life insurance companies must charge a fee associated with their risk related to the possibility of your mortality. Mortality risk, also known as risk of death, increases every day as you age. Life insurance companies increase the mortality cost for your policy's death benefit at every policy anniversary date. You never see this increase in cost reflected in your payment, because it is already built into your premium.[10]

Your payment is projected to remain level during the life of your policy. In general, life insurance policies are designed in this way to avoid an underfunding problem down the road. Theoretically speaking, with a level premium payment, you will overpay in the early years, and underpay in the later years.[11] The leveled-out premium design can and will break down if you don't pay enough premium, or, if your non-guaranteed policy underperforms.

There are literally hundreds of different non-guaranteed life insurance policies on the market today. All of these policies generally follow two basic designs: term life and universal life. Life insurance companies invent and re-create non-guaranteed hybrid policies based upon these two basic designs.

The people tasked with inventing a new hybrid policy are highly creative, and they find ways to make their product seem more attractive than the competition's. Most of the added design features layered over a basic design are not of great benefit to the consumer, as they generally add cost and risk to the policy which is then passed on to you, the policy owner.

The following are brief descriptions of these two basic policy designs, along with information about two popular design features that are commonly joined to a universal life design. These descriptions are specific to the non-guaranteed nature of each design and explain why they are ***considered a gamble***.

Term Life

A term is a pre-determined period of time. Most term life policies provide a guaranteed level-premium payment during the initial term, typically between 10 and 30 years after they are issued. After the initial term, your premium payment increases aggressively each year based upon your current age and unknown health status.

Most term policies are guaranteed to renew, even after the initial term is completed, until the insured reaches a certain age — such as 75. However, the life insurance company cannot require the insured to submit to underwriting at the end of the initial term. So, after the initial term is completed, the insured's health status is unknown to the life insurance company, and therefore, they cannot accurately assess their risk. As a result, mortality cost for an in-force term policy beyond its initial term is very expensive, often increasing the premium 5 to 6 times the initial term premium, and increasing more each year. For most people who keep their term policy beyond the initial term, the premium quickly becomes too expensive and the policy is cancelled.

Term life is not designed to provide a death benefit; it is designed to provide ***peace of mind*** over a specified period of time. If you have a term life policy which is in-force when you die, the death benefit will be paid out to your beneficiary. Nevertheless, term life is designed around the assumption that you will outlive the policy, or the policy will lapse in some other way.

There are two significant risks with a term life policy that make it a gamble:

1. You outlive your policy term. Hooray! You lost the bet! This is the bet you ***don't*** want to win. But what if you still need life insurance and your health declined over the years? Now you're stuck with a very expensive term life policy, and the premium will become even more expensive every year.

2. If you are ever more than 30 days late on a premium payment, ***for any reason***, your term life policy will lapse. Whether it's due to budget constraints, electronic funds payment failure, not receiving your payment notice because you moved and it wasn't forwarded properly to your new address — it doesn't matter. If you still want

financial protection after the term policy lapses, you are forced to apply for a new policy, and everything starts over again.

My advice: a term life policy plays an important role in providing affordable protection. The best use of term life is to blend a larger term life policy with a smaller, guaranteed cash-value policy such as participating whole life. This approach will significantly reduce the risks associated with term life. (See the appendix article: *The Balancing Act*℠ for more information.) If term life is the only type of life insurance you can afford, then buy it. At least you'll have peace of mind in case tragedy strikes.

Universal Life

The universal life policy design offers flexibility in premium payments and death benefit, and it may provide lifelong protection. Due to the flexible nature of the design, life insurance companies cannot guarantee the death benefit or a level-premium payment over your entire lifetime.

With traditional universal life, you have three adjustable control points within your policy:[12]

1. You may pay a higher premium than the amount set by the life insurance company, subject to IRS restrictions.[13]

2. You may pay a lower premium than the amount set by the life insurance company, as long as there is enough cash value in your policy to support your death benefit.

3. You may reduce the death benefit amount, subject to policy restrictions.

Traditional universal life provides an interest credit to your cash value, similar to a savings account. The interest credit is also flexible, and it is controlled by the life insurance company's board of directors. These are the people who are ultimately responsible for the financial performance of the life insurance company.

Every traditional universal life policy provides a declared minimum interest crediting rate that contractually obligates the life insurance company to credit at least that amount of interest to your cash value annually. Older policies, issued prior to 2009, generally guarantee between two and five percent annual interest. Policies issued since 2009 generally guarantee between zero and two percent annual interest. When this type of policy is purchased, the annual interest crediting rate will start out higher than the minimum amount guaranteed. Over time, the board of directors will reduce the interest credit until it reaches the minimum amount guaranteed in the policy; I have never seen an exception to this practice.

You must track the interest credit to your policy, and when it is reduced, respond by either paying a higher premium, or by reducing the death benefit to avoid a future underfunding problem. You must also understand that even with proper management, neither the death benefit nor the premium payment amount required to keep the policy are ever guaranteed.

There is one significant risk with a traditional universal life policy that makes it a gamble:

- Life gets busy and you don't properly manage your premium payments and/or death benefit in response to reductions in your interest credit. If this goes on long enough without an increase in premium payments or a reduction in the death benefit, your policy will lapse.

My advice: if you are willing to pay attention to your policy interest credit, and you can afford the premium amount that will support the death benefit at the minimum interest credit declared in the policy, this may be a good fit. It is the least risky of the "gambler" type of policies. There is another type of universal life policy I prefer called guaranteed universal life; which provides both a guaranteed level-premium payment and a guaranteed death benefit. The premium for a guaranteed universal life policy is also competitive with a traditional universal life policy.

A Personal Story – Universal Life Insurance

Before I entered the life insurance industry as a full-time career agent, I purchased a $100,000 universal life insurance policy. I was attracted to the policy because of the cash-value component, and the interest rate credit for the policy was substantially higher than I could get from a savings account at a bank. I also felt it was smart to have a long-term life insurance policy.

During the sales process I learned about the fluctuating interest rate, and at my option, I could pay more premium into the policy to offset the risk of a declining interest crediting rate. I was young, and qualified as a preferred risk, so the premium was affordable. I decided to pay a higher amount of premium than the amount set by the life insurance company.

Over time, the annual interest crediting rate declined until it reached it's guaranteed minimum of 4%. Today, I continue to pay the higher premium amount, and I have never been sorry for this decision.

Variable Life

A variable implies the unknown. That should give anyone pause before proceeding with a purchase. This is the wild west of life insurance. Variable life, by itself, is not a life insurance design. However, it adds powerful design features and deserves to be recognized here.

Variable refers to your cash value, which together with your premium payment, supports the cost of your death benefit over time. Theoretically, this is considered a "permanent" policy that may provide lifelong protection. Since the growth of the cash value is variable or unknown, neither the death benefit nor the premium payment amount can be guaranteed.

Variable life offers sub-accounts, similar to mutual funds, into which part of the premium you pay is deposited or invested. The sub-accounts are managed by professional investment firms, each of which charges its own separate fee for fund management, typically at least two percent annually.

The long-term health of a variable policy is completely dependent on the performance of these sub-accounts. A variable life policy offers no guarantees — zero — except the fees you will pay; those are always guaranteed!

There are too many risks with a variable life policy to list in this brief explanation. Here are the two biggest gambles:

1. Your chosen sub-accounts underperform. As your mortality cost rises in line with your age, and at the same time the cash value decreases due

to investment underperformance and fees, your policy will lapse. This risk increases significantly as you age.

2. You become spooked in a stock market downturn and withdraw the diminished cash value from your policy. Your policy will lapse.

My advice: unless you have a lot of money to throw at a variable life policy, stay away. Like any other need, the health of your life insurance policy should not be dependent upon the whims of stock markets.

A NON-GUARANTEED POLICY CAN BECOME A GUARANTEED NIGHTMARE

In October 2007, the company I represented assigned a large book of business to me. It was in a farming and ranching community, which at the time was not my strength. I had no experience in farming and ranching, but I knew a lot about insurance products and I was eager to learn about my new clients' needs.

My assistant began setting policy review appointments right away. I needed to find out what I had signed up for. Over a 20-year period, the area had gone through five different agents for this company. I soon learned I had been firmly planted in the center of a hornet's nest.

One of my first review appointments was with an older couple who owned a successful sheep ranch. They were glad my assistant called because they had some questions about their life insurance policy. It was an older, variable universal life insurance policy they started in the early 1990s, about 25 years prior. They made their payments faithfully but had taken a small loan from the cash value of their policy that had not yet been paid back. A couple of years before their account was assigned to me, they started receiving letters from the life insurance company stating they might need to pay more premium to keep their policy, and they were concerned. The prior agent (just before me) told them not to worry about it. "The policy will turn around in time; they always do," he had told them. My new clients wanted to know if it would be worthwhile to pay off the small loan. That's where the conversation started.

After going over their concerns, I set a follow-up appointment with them to discuss specifics after I had a chance to look into their situation through our home office. About a week later, they came to my office for the follow-up appointment. Unfortunately, the news was disturbing. The premium requirement to keep the policy healthy was unreasonable, and other policy options were very expensive for the amount of life insurance they wanted, since they were now well into their 60s. According to this couple, none of my five predecessors explained how this policy actually worked. They were just told it would grow with the stock market, without a word about how the mortality cost would increase each year, not to mention the other associated fees.

Needless to say, they were very upset. They wrote a letter to the life insurance company explaining that they only now felt like they understood their policy. In the letter, they also requested that the life insurance company allow some kind of compromise, due to the circumstances. Since a life insurance policy is a legal contract, the result, unfortunately, was already baked in. The life insurance company could not compromise without creating a favorable bias, which is frowned upon by regulators. This couple, now at retirement, had paid over $120,000 into a now worthless non-guaranteed policy.

Indexed Life

Indexed means limited, in the context of life insurance. Similar to variable life, indexed life is not a life insurance design. Nevertheless, it adds powerful design features and deserves to be recognized here.

This one is intensely complex. Though the following description is brief and over-simplified, it should satisfy any basic curiosity of the risks which lurk within this policy design.

"Let me see if I'm misunderstanding this correctly..."

Indexed refers to your cash value, which together with your premium payment supports the cost of your death benefit over time. Theoretically, this is considered a "permanent" policy that may provide lifelong protection. Since the growth of the cash value is indexed, or limited, based upon the indexing rules for the policy, neither the death benefit nor the premium payment can be guaranteed. The indexing credits for your policy are set by your chosen life insurance company's board of directors , and generally, they can be changed at any time.

Indexed life typically offers a small menu of investment strategies, one of which is usually the S&P 500. Part of your premium payment is deposited into your chosen investment strategy; this is your policy cash value. With indexed life, the growth of your cash value is limited using three moving parts:

1. Cap rate with a guaranteed floor – The life insurance company guarantees you will not lose anything on the investment side by providing a zero percent floor; your cash value will never decline due to a downturn in the stock market. It also sets a growth cap that it can change, up or down, whenever it chooses. Let's say the cap rate is 6 percent. If your chosen investment is the S&P 500, and it grows by 12 percent one year, your cash value will be credited the cap rate of 6 percent. But it doesn't stop there.

2. Participation rate – The life insurance company also decides how much you can participate in the growth. If your participation rate is 70 percent, your cash value will be credited with 70 percent of the 6 percent cap, which equals 4.2 percent in this example. But it doesn't stop there.

3. Point-to-point interest crediting measurement – You choose how your indexed crediting is applied. You may choose an annual measurement of the S&P 500, or, you may choose an averaging technique called "monthly point-to-point" to smooth out the final result.

There are many risks with an indexed life policy. Here's the biggest gamble:

- In your later years, the life insurance company reduces the cap rate and participation rate to a point that your premium payment and cash value cannot keep up with your rising mortality cost. If you don't increase your premium payment, or reduce your death benefit, your policy will lapse.

My advice: If this short description is over your head, run away from indexed life. If you are attracted to the safety features that prevent investment loss, keep in mind, you will still be charged for your mortality cost and other associated fees. So, while you may not take an investment loss in a bad stock market year, you will still experience a loss to your cash value.

Points to Ponder

1. Would you consider getting into a non-guaranteed mortgage? Let's say you made all of your scheduled monthly payments, initially set by the lender, over the full term of the mortgage. But then your lender informs you the loan is not yet paid in full. You may need to pay for several more years. Does that seem enticing?

2. Term life is easy on the budget. However, if you are willing and able to pay more for a life insurance policy that guarantees a ***full refund*** of all premium paid, with a guaranteed death benefit and a guaranteed level-premium during the term, return of premium term life insurance may be the best option for you.

THE BOTTOM LINE

If you don't understand it, don't buy it. If you can't afford it, don't buy it. If it requires babysitting and you are not willing to actively manage it over a long period of time, don't buy it.

If you can afford a permanent, cash value life insurance policy, then buy one that is simple and guaranteed. Life insurance is your family's financial lifeline to secure their needs if you die. The health of your life insurance policy should not be tied up in a gamble. Keep risk where it belongs; with ***wise*** investments.

If you cannot afford a guaranteed cash value life insurance policy, then buy a term life policy. You can buy a guaranteed cash value life insurance policy in the future when you can afford it.

Whether you go with a temporary solution just for peace of mind, or a permanent lifelong solution, or even if you purchase both, buy life insurance for the life insurance, not for potential financial growth. Potential financial growth is called an investment, and sometimes they don't go so well.

From Non-Guaranteed to Guaranteed

What if you have a non-guaranteed cash value policy, such as universal life, variable life or indexed life? Can you do anything to change course? Yes! Under IRS code, section 1035, you can exchange the cash value in your non-guaranteed policy into a new guaranteed participating whole life

policy, or any other guaranteed cash value life insurance policy.[14] Similar to exchanging equity from the home you sold to the home you just bought, this exchange of cash value is ***not*** a taxable event, and a guaranteed cash value life insurance policy will place you in a much stronger long-term position with your life insurance plan.

What's Next

Want to get the most out of a life insurance plan without blowing up your budget? You may be surprised to learn that simplicity, together with strong guarantees, is the best and most cost-effective solution for most people. Journey on for more details.

CHAPTER SEVEN

The Ugly Duckling and the Cheap Fix

The Story of the Participating Whole Life Insurance Policy

DO YOU REMEMBER THE story of the Ugly Duckling? It is a beautiful tale of transformation. A mother duck is raising her brood of ducklings, but one of them is different. It is awkward and ugly; an unattractive misfit. The other ducklings tease and chide the ugly duckling to no end. As the story goes, the young misfit, who had been misidentified as a duck, grows over time into a great swan — the most beautiful and graceful of all water fowl!

I have always loved this classic tale for its endearing humanity. Its simple and timeless message resonates with anyone who has ever felt out of place, or misunderstood. And, believe it or not, it is also the story of the participating whole life insurance policy.

In recent decades, whole life has become the ugly duckling amongst life insurance products. The reasons are simple: it's more expensive to the budget, making it ugly; and it's slow to grow, making it a misfit. In today's financial products world, consumers demand more for their purchasing dollars. We want everything financial to offer reasonably strong growth potential. That's a rational expectation if we're talking about a 401(k), an IRA, or some other type of long-term investment account involving some risk. But it's not a good fit for life insurance. As stock markets have increased in popularity, consumers have begun to apply investment principals and expectations to financial products that never had a history in stock markets.

Life insurance companies caught on to this consumer trend in the 1980s and started inventing products to fulfill consumer demand. Essentially, life insurance companies have instituted a Frankenstein-design approach to life insurance policies for the purpose of attracting consumer spending. These newer products create a ton of profit for life insurance companies due to their non-guaranteed designs (see the previous chapter, *Beware the Gambler*).

But life insurance, by its very nature, is not on the strong-growth side of the financial product ledger. It is ***meant*** to be slow, steady and safe because it's life insurance! If your job is walking the high wire at the circus, you need the safety net below to be strong, steady and stable. Though the net is vital to your safety and security, and therefore it is an important part of your act, it is boring and goes largely unnoticed by almost everybody. Nevertheless, it's your protection, and if you ever need it, ***everybody*** will be grateful it was there.

Participating whole life is, hands down, the highest quality life insurance policy, financial safety net or financial back-up plan, on the market. Given enough time, it is also the least expensive to own. Many participating whole life policies reach breakeven between 12 and 15 years. At that point, you begin to make a profit. Participating whole life is the only life insurance product that can offer this type of return ***and*** provide a guaranteed death benefit together with a guaranteed level-premium payment.

Participating Whole Life

"Participating" means participation in favorable performance or profits, through dividend payments. When a life insurance company posts an annual profit, a policy dividend is declared.[15] As an owner of a participating whole life policy, you share in the annual profit by receiving a dividend based on a few factors, one of them being your policy's accumulated cash value. In the early years, your cash value, and therefore your dividend, will be low. As your cash value grows over time, your dividend payments will also grow; they will eventually represent a significant amount of money. While dividend payments are not guaranteed, historically speaking, participating whole life policies have consistently delivered annual dividends to policy owners.

There are several ways to receive your dividend:

- Cash – you will receive an annual dividend check.
- Reduced premium – your dividend will be credited as premium and will reduce your premium payment for that year.
- Paid-up additions – your dividend will pay in-full for additional life insurance coverage; the additional life insurance will also qualify for future dividends.
- At interest – your dividend is deposited into a savings account with your life insurance company and it grows at interest.

Seems like a no-brainer, right? But then you see the price tag. The greatest obstacle to the purchase of a ***large*** whole life policy is affordability. Most people cannot afford to place all of their life insurance needs into whole life, regardless of the benefits. But there is a way to enjoy the benefits of participating whole life without blowing up your budget.

The Cheap Fix

Buyer's remorse is something we all endure from time to time. "That ice cream looked so good, but it's not what I expected. Why didn't I ask for a sample taste before I bought it?" Or, "I really love the look of these shoes, but they hurt my feet after just a short time. I wish I had been more careful before I bought them."

Experiences like these are common. We make assumptions, and we let our emotions guide our purchasing behavior. While shoes that don't quite fit and ice cream that doesn't taste how we expected would be disappointing, these experiences don't impact us much. Ice cream and shoes are small purchases. Our buyer's remorse subsides quickly and we move on, hopefully a little wiser. But with life insurance, you could commit many thousands of dollars to a policy before discovering you purchased the wrong product for your situation.

Nearly everybody needs life insurance. Most people appreciate the value of whole life insurance after just a small amount of unbiased research. So, how do you obtain an ***affordable*** whole life policy that fits your needs ***and*** will grow enough over time so you can receive all of your money back?

I created a strategy called *The Balancing Act*℠. It's a smaller whole life policy to cover your final expense needs, joined with a large term life policy to cover your temporary needs. Over time, the cash value accumulation from the guaranteed interest credit and the non-guaranteed dividends in your whole life policy will grow to cover the cost of both policies. This creates several future options:

1. Later in life, if you don't need life insurance any longer, you can cash-in your whole life policy and recoup the entire cost of your life insurance over all of those years.[16]

2. If you still need life insurance, just keep the whole life policy and continue paying the premium.

3. If you want to keep your whole life policy, but you don't want the payment any longer, simply reduce the death benefit to a guaranteed paid-up policy. This allows you to keep the policy for your final expenses without needing to pay any more premium.

There are many desirable options that stem from a smart plan.

Imagine paying a life insurance premium for 10, 20, or even 30 years, and have nothing to show for it. What an unnecessary loss! Talk about buyer's remorse! But if you include a small participating whole life policy that builds equity over the years, you could recoup all of the money you paid for both your whole life ***and*** term life policies over that same period of time. It's an "ugly duckling" life insurance plan that transforms into a great financial swan!

My Personal Ugly Duckling Story

As I matured in my life insurance career, I came to realize that participating whole life is the highest quality life insurance product available. Over the course of my career, working with many clients who have owned policies for decades, I've had the opportunity to observe how different policy types perform over a long period of time. In my experience, a good-quality participating whole life policy always out-performed every other policy type — without exception.

Soon after I came to this realization, I purchased my own $100,000 participating whole life policy. I also own a large term life policy, and a $100,000 traditional universal life policy that I purchased many years ago. As time goes by, and my financial protection needs change, I will make changes to these policies to fit my needs.

Although I once owned variable life insurance, I will never again purchase that type of policy, knowing what I know now. Nor will I ever consider an indexed life insurance policy for myself.

Slow and Steady Wins the Life Insurance Race

Another one of my favorite tales is the Tortoise and the Hare. With life insurance, you must be the tortoise. Similar to a marathon, slow and steady is the best strategy for a life insurance plan — and the tortoise wins every time. Don't let the life insurance company out-tortoise you!

Today, many people buy a non-guaranteed life insurance policy from an agent who has been trained and encouraged to sell non-guaranteed policies. Then the life insurance company just sits back and waits for you to lose patience. And you will lose patience because the non-guaranteed design will eventually begin to work against you. Finally, you cancel the policy and the life insurance company escapes the obligation to pay the death benefit, resulting in a huge profit for the company and its investors.

With participating whole life, your premium never increases, your death benefit is guaranteed, and your cash value will grow on a guaranteed schedule with added dividends as the life insurance company posts profits. The life insurance company will still make a profit from your policy, it will just be a much smaller profit. And you saunter away with money in your pocket. Remember, you're a tortoise!

THE BOTTOM LINE

Life insurance, as a concept, represents a financial safety net to your loved ones in case of death. A financial safety net requires stability and strength over a long period of time to be effective. It is wise to let your financial safety net do the job it was intended to do, rather than expecting it to also act like an investment. Secure your family's financial safety net through strong guarantees, and control the cost by blending participating whole life with term life. This will result in a smart approach to high-quality coverage at an affordable price.

1. Purchase a small participating whole life policy to cover your final expenses, in the likely event you live to an older age.
2. Purchase a large term life policy to cover your temporary protection needs, such as income replacement, debt payoff, etc.
3. In the future, reassess your needs when your term life policy ends.
    - If you don't need life insurance any longer, recoup your premium costs by cashing in your participating whole life policy.
    - If you need life insurance for final expenses, but don't want the payment, reduce your whole life death benefit to a paid-up policy. Your participating whole life death benefit will continue to grow as dividends are paid into your policy each year. Or you can receive the dividends in the form of an annual payment. Now the life insurance company is paying ***you***!
    - Other options are also available.

What's Next

You now know the strategy to win your life insurance marathon. But what are the specifics and how does The Balancing Act work? Continue on to learn more.

Questions about anything covered in this chapter?
We have answers — info@simplislife.com or (888) 385.1711
www.simplislife.com

APPENDIX

Take Action

You know your budget range

You know your range of protection need

You know which policy types are best for you

Let's Build Your Plan!

The BALANCING ACT℠
A Strategy for Success

BALANCE: WITHOUT IT, we fall. And it's true whether we're standing up on our feet, or putting together a life insurance plan. If we place too much emphasis on one side; we wobble, we strain, we flail about — and finally, we fall. This article describes a strategy that will place you in a strong and stable position to be balanced and successful with your life insurance planning. And the best part is, it's simple, cost-effective and easy to implement!

Success with life insurance begins with an open mind. Over the past several decades, a great debate has raged on about the different types of life insurance. During this period, the two opposing sides have become increasingly extreme and have developed strong, passionate opinions. "Buy investment-grade life insurance and take advantage of market gains!" is what you hear on one side. "NO! Buy term and invest the difference!" is what you hear on the other side. This opinionated back-and-forth quarreling leaves consumers confused about who's right and who's wrong.

The truth is, no one is right and no one is wrong. Individual needs are diverse. And your needs will even change throughout your life. Life insurance products are also diverse; there is a policy out there for every need. With the right plan, life insurance can accomplish some amazing financial feats. It can also deliver disappointment if you're ill-informed.

So, how do you create a ***winning*** life insurance plan? Let's start with the things you control:

- Accepting reality – Everyone dies; it's guaranteed. Your death will cause expenses — also guaranteed. By accepting these realities, you will begin to think in terms of covering expenses related to your death regardless of when it happens. For most people, it makes sense to have a lot of protection when raising a family, and/or you have heavy financial obligations; and less protection when entering retirement, with fewer financial obligations.

- Product selection – When you purchase a life insurance policy, you are entering into a legal contract with a huge life insurance company. Place yourself in the best position possible by purchasing products with ***strong guarantees***.

- A reasonable budget – Being strategic with the dollars set aside to protect your loved ones is vital to a successful outcome. It's tempting to fall into the "cheap" trap. Cheap isn't a bad thing, but if all of your protection dollars are dumped into the "cheap" side, you will be out of balance, and you'll be disappointed in the end.

Now, how do you provide the financial needs related to your death in the most cost-effective way, regardless of when you die?

It's Not One or the Other

Generally speaking, there are two opposing viewpoints when it comes to product choice.

1. Term life insurance offers an inexpensive option to provide peace of mind. You can cover your entire need at a very low cost. It does not, however, offer any living benefits or equity build-up. It doesn't protect you against a temporary loss of income, which may ultimately cause your term policy to lapse due to non-payment. Also, most people outlive their term policy. It's tough to look back over 20 or 30 years of faithful payments and have nothing to show for it.

2. Participating whole life insurance offers a guaranteed death benefit along with numerous living benefits. It can provide a financial safety net along with easy access to equity for a future financial need, while the insured is still living. Over time, it can pay for itself through tax-favored equity build-up. And if you keep the policy long enough, you can even end up making a profit with participating whole life.[17] Yet, realistically most people cannot afford the premium for a ***large*** death benefit participating whole life insurance policy.

For many people, term vs. participating whole life presents a dilemma:

> "Should I just sign-up for pure protection for the amount of life insurance I need, knowing I'll probably never use it and feel like I'm throwing my money away?, OR, should I sign up for less life insurance than I need, and pay what I can afford into a policy that will at least allow me to recoup my premium payments in the future?"

These questions tend to set up a false premise of a mutually exclusive choice — an "either/or" situation. But the opposite is true. For most people, the answer is simple: **CHOOSE BOTH**. Financially speaking, your death could mean a lost income to your dependents, or, if you die later in life, it will create some final expenses. Why not set up your life insurance plan in a way that will satisfy your loved one's financial needs whether you die young *or* old?

Here's the logic for choosing both and implementing *The Balancing Act*℠ strategy:

1. Statistically speaking, you will live a long life. If you have a participating whole life policy in-force at the time you die to cover your final expenses, your loved ones will be in a strong financial position to handle all of your final needs. Starting a participating whole life insurance policy while you are young and in good health is the most cost-effective way to handle your final expenses. And your loved ones who take on this responsibility for you will admire your preparation, and appreciate your thoughtfulness.[18]

2. If you're the exception to the rule and you die young — while you're raising a family, have debt, and other heavy financial obligations — you'll have that covered with a large amount of term life. You will also have a participating whole life policy for your final expenses. In this way, your family will have the ability to emotionally heal in a healthy way, transition to their new family dynamic with dignity, and retain their independence.

3. But if you're like most people, you will outlive your term life policy. At that time, you may decide that you are financially strong enough to forego all of your life insurance. In this scenario, you may wish to cancel your participating whole life policy, and in many cases, the cash value you receive will be enough to cover all of your premium cost for both the participating whole life policy **and** the term life policy.

4. If, on the other hand, you still need some life insurance after your term life policy expires, you can still keep your whole life policy. You can even reduce the death benefit to a paid-up policy. This will provide you with a final expenses death benefit, with no further premium payment obligation.

With a balanced life insurance plan, whether you live a long life, or you leave a young family behind, you're covered appropriately. And you retain control over the flexibility of your planning as your needs change. By using *The Balancing Act*℠ strategy, whether you live a long life or not, you get something out of your purchase. And that is satisfying.

In my experience, most people are happiest when they purchase one type of policy that addresses the short-term and mid-term needs: term life insurance. And another type of policy for the long-term needs, such as final expenses: participating whole life insurance. This balanced approach to life insurance planning provides the highest rate of satisfaction for most people.

How to Create Your Own Balanced Life Insurance Plan

Anyone who is raising a family, providing an income, or has lots of debt, needs a lot of financial protection. At the same time, most of us have a limited budget. If this sounds like you, creating a life insurance plan is actually quite easy. It can be broken down into three simple steps:

1. Decide how much money is available in your budget for life insurance premium, rather than establishing a pre-determined limit. This step is not about how much you want to spend, it's about how much you have available to spend. Understanding this will help you create a sustainable plan. (See chapter two, *It's a Budget Thing*)

2. Decide how much life insurance you want to have when you are elderly for your final expenses. This is usually between $25,000 and $100,000. The younger you are, the more you need due to future inflation.

3. Decide how much life insurance you need if you die tomorrow (Use the Life Insurance Calculator). https://www.simplislife.com/calculator

When you understand your life insurance need and your available budget, you're in control. Now it's just a matter of finding the right balance of term life and participating whole life insurance. Both your age and coverage need play an important role in determining a healthy balance. For example:

- If you're under 40 years old, and you need $1,100,000 of total life insurance protection, consider a $100,000 participating whole life policy and $1,000,000 of term life.

- If you're between 40 and 55 years old, and you need $775,000 of total life insurance protection, consider a $75,000 participating whole life policy and $700,000 of term life.

- If you're between 56 and 67 years old, and you need $300,000 of total life insurance protection, consider a $50,000 participating whole life policy and $250,000 of term life.

- If you're over 67 years old and you need $125,000 of total life insurance protection, consider a $25,000 participating whole life policy and $100,000 of term life.

Everyone's situation is unique. These guidelines provide a starting point to determine the best balance for you. And the fact is, no one will ever understand your situation better than you, so no one is better equipped than you to create the best balance.

Principals of Protection

You may remember way back in chapter one, *Plan B for Back-Up*, we reviewed the three principles of protection: security, options and performance. How does *The Balancing Act*℠ measure up to these important principles?

1. Security – Participating whole life offers the strongest guarantees available amongst life insurance products. Term life, with a guaranteed level premium, offers strong guarantees during the initial term, conditioned upon your on-time premium payments. The cash value within a whole life policy provides the redundancy to protect your plan should you encounter an unexpected financial speed bump, such as a temporary period of unemployment. The cash value can be used to pay the premium for both the whole life policy and the term life policy until you are able to get back on your financial feet. You can then resume payment for both policies from the income earned at your new

job. This way, your loved ones will be protected during a financially stressful and vulnerable period, and you will be able to continue your original life insurance plan well into the future.

2. Options – A participating whole life policy will flex to allow for your changing needs when you are older, for final expenses. You can reduce the death benefit to a paid-up policy if you wish, so you won't need to pay any further premium, and the life insurance company will actually pay you the annual dividend. The greater area of flexibility can be built-in to your term life as a design feature called "laddering" (see The Life Insurance Ladder, page 84).

3. Performance – A healthy balance of participating whole life and term life will result in high-quality guaranteed protection, and can provide the opportunity to recoup your entire cost, for both policies, after a 20-year to 30-year period. It will also be more affordable than other comparable plans. The payment of your premium is the only management requirement to achieve your goals with this strategy. This is as low-maintenance as it gets with life insurance.

With *The Balancing Act*℠ strategy, you will have strong guarantees, flexibility and — at your option — you can recoup all the premium you paid. The cash value in the whole life policy provides the redundancy necessary to eliminate any single point of failure in this plan. Clearly, *The Balancing Act* passes the Principals of Protection test with three out of three bright gold stars! How does your current life insurance plan measure up?

The Life Insurance Ladder

Carefully navigating up and down a ladder is a familiar concept in career management, parenting teenagers, and the physical act itself. Successful ladder navigation requires a healthy mix of courage, wisdom and patience. But even the most careful will run into the occasional "oh crap!" moments. The overall goal is to remain confidently stable on the ladder, wherever you are positioned. So, what does successful ladder navigation look like in the world of life insurance?

For most of us, our financial protection need is greatest when we are young and raising a family. Let's say you're married with three children, ages 10, 7 and 5. You've calculated your protection need at $1,100,000. Here's how laddering looks in this situation:

- **$100,000** of participating whole life for your final expenses, in the likely event you live a long life.

- **$500,000 of 30-year,** guaranteed level-premium term life. This will be there to protect your children while they are dependents, as well as your surviving spouse for at least a decade after your children are raised and on their own.

- **$250,000 of 20-year,** guaranteed level-premium term life. This will be there to protect your family until your youngest child is 25 years old.

- **$250,000 of 10-year,** guaranteed level-premium term life. This will be there to protect your family until your youngest child is 15 years old.

As time passes, each of the term life policies will naturally end as your financial obligations diminish. As your protection declines, your overall premium expense will also decline. After 30 years, you will be left with a very valuable participating whole life policy that you may keep in its current form, cash-in to recoup your premium expenses, or reduce the death benefit to a paid-up policy for your final expenses.

This is one of many options available for this family dynamic. You will be the best judge of how much protection your family needs and during which periods of time, as you look into the future. This example is provided to help you understand the concept of laddering. Your situation may differ.

Management of multiple life insurance policies is about the same as one life insurance policy, as long as all policies have strong guarantees. It is just a matter of setting up a separate file for each policy in your file cabinet, be it a physical one or a digital version. Everything else remains the same. And believe it or not, one application process can be used for multiple policies!

COOL TOOLS

Try these helpful tools to develop your balanced life insurance plan:

- Discover which types of policies will work best for you: **Policy***Quest*℠ uses a light algorithm to help you understand the best type of life insurance policy for your situation. (https://www.simplislife.com/policy-quest-intro/)
- Calculate your total need: *Life Insurance Calculator* (https://www.simplislife.com/calculator/)
- *Get a Quote* from many different life insurance companies. (https://www.simplislife.com/quoter/)

THE BOTTOM LINE

Nearly everything in life requires a healthy balance to achieve desirable results; life insurance is no exception. By using a balanced approach, you will place yourself and your loved ones in the best position possible for long-term success with your life insurance planning.

Note of Clarification

Throughout this appendix article, I have used participating whole life as the cash value product of choice for *The Balancing Act*℠ strategy. You may use whichever cash value or "permanent" life insurance policy you wish for this strategy, as long as the policy can build up significant cash value. Guaranteed universal life is not a good fit for this strategy, as it is not designed to generate a large cash value over time. Any policy with a variable design component is not appropriate for this strategy, and policies with an indexed design component should be used with caution. Variable designs and indexed designs depend — at least in part — on timing of the underlying investments associated with their cash value growth, or their cash value decline (see chapter six, *Beware the Gambler*).

Participating whole life is my personal and professional preference due to its strong guarantees and its ability to deliver significant cash value growth on a pre-determined schedule. Participating whole life is the only life insurance product that allows you to have complete control over the outcome, while at the same time, delivering significant cash value growth.

Do you need help with your balanced life insurance plan?
Questions about anything covered in this chapter?
We can help — info@simplislife.com or (888) 385.1711
www.simplislife.com

Special Needs

SOMETIMES THERE IS A fine line between duty and love. When raising a special needs child, especially into adulthood, that fine line is often the common thread between these two very real human emotions that keeps a family caregiver going. Many family members are not able to cope as a long-term caregiver, and in those cases, there are government sponsored homes with paid staff to care for special needs individuals. Caregiver burnout is real. These supportive options can help to promote a healthy and balanced relationship with a special needs loved one.

I have a special needs family member; my brother-in-law, DJ. He has lived with me and my wife (his sister) for seven years. We deeply love and care for him, and we attend to his needs. But some days — well, it can be very challenging.

Without a doubt, day-to-day living is full of ups and downs, repetitive conversations, and other patience-building experiences. And that doesn't even take into account the requirements of the various state government agencies and the massive amount of paperwork that goes along with it! It can be a true burden. Gratefully, daily work programs and respite care are available to provide relief to caregivers, and give the special needs family member an opportunity to form relationships with others in the community.

When a special needs loved one lives in a group home, or host home, staff members of that business attend to the needs of these clients. Even though government funded programs like these provide for life's essentials, they do not provide for anything beyond simple dignity, and even that is questionable in some situations.

Financial Protection Now and Later

Financial support protection through life insurance for a special needs minor child is similar to that of other children, with perhaps some additional expenses depending on the disability. Nevertheless, the concept is the same: family lifestyle protection, debt payoff, etc.

When a special needs child reaches adulthood, financial support protection through life insurance breaks down into two lines of thought:

1. When the parents pass away, the state government will take care of their disabled child's needs. There is no need for further financial support.

2. When the parents pass away, a life insurance death benefit can help to financially support their disabled child. The state government will certainly provide support, but with financial support from a death benefit, other options become available through supplemental support to provide an improved situation for their child's care and needs.

Most parents and other family members want their special needs loved one to have the opportunity to participate in life-enriching activities beyond just the basics. Life insurance is by far the best financial product to deliver supplemental support over the lifetime of a special needs family member.

Special Needs Trust

One of the challenges to providing financial support for a disabled, dependent adult is the Medicaid rulebook (Medi-Cal in California). The best solution for this challenge is to create a Special Needs Trust, sometimes called a Supplemental Needs Trust. If you are considering a Special Needs Trust for your loved one, seek proper legal guidance from a licensed and reputable estate attorney.

Assuming you either have such a Trust, or intend to create one, your special needs child will be able to receive financial support from a life insurance death benefit payable to the Trust, without infringing upon the government-sponsored benefits necessary for proper care.

For most special needs situations, the life insurance policy is intended to provide ***supplemental*** support. Government benefits will provide the basics, for survival, while the death benefit from a life insurance policy will fund the Trust for the purpose of providing additional needed support.

A Personal Story – **DJ's Boy Scout Jamboree Trip**

At the age of 46, DJ is an active Boy Scout with a local special needs troop. In 2001, he had the opportunity to travel to Fort A.P. Hill, Virginia for the national Boy Scout Jamboree. His troop also visited New York City and Boston. He was able to have this experience because he had funding available to pay for the trip. Without this additional funding, this wouldn't have been possible for him, as government programs don't provide support outside of basic needs. To this day, he still talks about

this trip, and shows his Jamboree photo album to people who visit. It's a cherished memory for him, and we all deserve to have a few of those.

ABLE Account

If a Trust is not a good fit for your family, there is another alternative: an ABLE account.

In 2014, the federal Achieving a Better Life Experience (ABLE) Act was passed into law. Since then, states have started to adopt this Act in various forms. An ABLE account allows funds for the benefit of a disabled adult to be deposited and held outside the Medicaid/Medi-Cal rules.

This is a great program, and helps to address many of the financial challenges for the special needs community. The regulations that govern this program can be different from state to state. The annual deposit restriction for ABLE accounts is tied to the federal gift tax exclusion, making this option less desirable for deposits in excess of the gift tax exclusion limit. For more information, visit: the ABLE National Resource Center website (https://www.ablenrc.org/).

How Much Is Enough?

The amount of coverage you select for your disabled child's lifelong supplemental support depends on two factors:

1. The current age of your special needs child.
2. How much annual financial support you wish to provide.

For example, if your child is 25 years old and you wish to provide at least $2,000 of annual supplemental financial support when you pass away, you will want to obtain between $50,000 and $100,000 of life insurance protection for this need. If your child is older, you may need less life insurance protection for this need.

The ***two greatest unknowns*** for selecting the right amount of coverage are:

1. Your date of death.
2. Your child's date of death.

With this type of need, it is always wise to overfund rather than underfund. With proper management of these funds, your child will have the financial ability to enjoy positive life experiences that government-sponsored programs won't provide.

Financial Protection for Special Needs

Special needs individuals are permanently disabled. Generally speaking, the disability began at birth or during early childhood — with exceptions, of course. With this in mind, you should create a life insurance plan with strong guarantees. Here are your best options:

1. Participating whole life – With its strong guarantees and lifelong design, whole life is the best solution. It is also the most expensive.
2. Term life – Term life is easiest on the budget; however, it provides only temporary guarantees for financial protection, and a permanent disability is a lifelong situation.

These product options can create a dilemma if there isn't enough money in the budget for whole life but you want to provide guaranteed, lifelong protection. Let's look at a few creative options.

Survivorship Whole Life

This may be a good fit if your special needs child has reached adulthood and you do not currently have a life insurance plan in place for this need. Survivorship whole life covers the lives of both parents, and pays the death benefit when the last-surviving parent dies. Your premium rate is established using a blended approach to underwriting. In other words, even if one parent has serious health issues, you can still obtain a policy with an affordable premium.

Convertible Term Life

This is a great way to control the cost of insurance and still provide lifelong protection, especially if your special needs child is still a minor. Create a protection plan around *The Balancing Act*℠ model. Before your term life policy reaches the end of its initial term, convert it to a participating whole life policy for an amount that will provide for the supplemental support of your special needs child. The conversion process does not require any underwriting, so your health at the time of conversion is not an issue. This is the best solution if your current budget will not allow for additional whole life for this need.

Guaranteed Universal Life

Guaranteed universal life provides a death benefit guarantee and a level-premium guarantee, as long as your premium is paid on time. Technically, it is a cash value policy, but it does not develop very much cash value over time. This policy design helps to control your cost of insurance, but it does not provide an effective cash-out feature to recoup your cost unless you add a Return of Premium rider. The premium for guaranteed universal life will be more than term life, but less than whole life. It will provide a guaranteed death benefit for lifelong protection at a more affordable price point. Unfortunately, it is not very forgiving if a premium payment is missed.

Life Insurance for a Special Needs Individual

In many cases, you can obtain an affordable life insurance policy to cover final expenses for a special needs loved one. Many life insurance companies offer policies with relaxed underwriting guidelines. As long as your special needs family member does not have a terminal illness, you should be able to find an affordable solution.

THE BOTTOM LINE

Every human being deserves the opportunity for their life to be as fulfilling as possible. Special needs individuals are perhaps the most vulnerable members of society, and therefore depend on their loved ones to look out for not only their needs, but also their quality of life. There are practical and affordable solutions to guarantee your special needs child will have funds available to not just survive, but also to enjoy life as much as possible.

Questions about anything covered in this chapter?
We have answers — info@simplislife.com or (888) 385.1711
www.simplislife.com

Disclosures & Disclaimers

No Legal Advice Offered
I am not a licensed attorney. Any guidance in this book should not be construed as legal advice. Any opinions expressed in this book regarding Wills, Trusts, bankruptcy or any other subject matter within the purview of the legal profession, and/or legal representation, should be referred to a properly licensed and reputable attorney.

How Is My Life Insurance Policy Protected If My Chosen Life Insurance Company Becomes Insolvent?
The Life & Health Insurance Guarantee Association for your state works with your state's regulators to protect consumers from losing policy death benefits and cash value when a life insurance company becomes insolvent.

Here is a brief explanation from the National Organization of Life & Health Insurance Guaranty Associations:

ROLE OF THE GUARANTY ASSOCIATIONS

> State life and health insurance guaranty associations are state entities (in all 50 states as well as Puerto Rico and the District of Columbia) created to protect policyholders of an insolvent insurance company. All insurance companies (with limited exceptions) licensed to sell life or health insurance in a state must be members of that state's guaranty association.

Guaranteed Coverage

While laws governing maximum limits and types of policies covered vary from state to state, most states are consistent with the NAIC Model Act and provide coverage at least in the amounts specified below. Check your state association's website to confirm the applicable benefit levels in your state.

$300,000 in life insurance death benefits

$100,000 in cash surrender or withdrawal values for life insurance.[19]

Website content used with permission.

If you would like to learn more, please go to the Life & Health Insurance Guarantee Association website for your state. While there, you will be able to confirm the minimum amounts of death benefit and withdrawal value protected from a life insurance company insolvency. You will also be able to learn more about how this program works.

Life Insurance Descriptions

Any description of a life insurance product in this book is over-simplified for the purpose of helping the reader understand those parts of a life insurance policy that are most pertinent to consumers. The same policy type can exist in many variations. Also, life insurance companies often create policy design features and riders which change how a life insurance policy performs. It is impossible to discuss all of these various options completely and thoroughly in this consumer-centric format. For this reason, the author has provided brief summary descriptions of the more common life insurance products that are offered by life insurance companies.

Whom Do I Contact If I Have A Concern About My Life Insurance Policy?

If your life insurance company cannot resolve a concern, you can contact the Department of Insurance or the Office of Insurance Commissioner for your state. These are the regulatory bodies that oversee the insurance industry. Contact information for your state's insurance regulator will be included in your policy, usually in the Buyer's Guide section or on the policy specifications page. You may also search online for your state's Department of Insurance contact information.

Endnotes

1 Sears cancels group life for retirees: https://www.chicagotribune.com/business/ct-biz-sears-ends-life-insurance-benefits-20190326-story.html

2 Premium payments for a whole life policy and a *guaranteed* universal life policy remain level for as long as you own the policy. For term life insurance with a guaranteed level premium, the premium payment remains level for the initial term of the policy. All other policy types *do not offer* guaranteed level-premium payments.

3 If you purchase a guaranteed level-premium term policy, your payment amount will not increase during the initial term. If you purchase a guaranteed premium cash-value policy, such as whole life or guaranteed universal life, your payment amount is locked-in and can never increase. If you purchase a non-guaranteed policy such as, universal life, variable life or indexed life, your payment amount is never guaranteed and could increase over time.

4 The rules which govern bankruptcy procedures may vary, depending upon your situation and jurisdiction. Consult a licensed and reputable bankruptcy attorney for further information on this topic.

5 Social Security Benefits Planner: Survivors: https://www.ssa.gov/planners/survivors/ifyou.html. Social Security Benefits Planner: Planning For Your Survivors: https://www.ssa.gov/planners/survivors/onyourown.html

6 Fast Facts and Figures About Social Security, 2019: https://www.ssa.gov/policy/docs/chartbooks/fast_facts/2019/fast_facts19.pdf

7 All human behavior can be reduced to 'four basic emotions': https://www.bbc.com/news/uk-scotland-glasgow-west-26019586

8 Average expenses related to a traditional funeral and a cremation with services: https://www.nfda.org/news/statistics/. A helpful checklist: https://www.consumer.ftc.gov/articles/0301-funeral-costs-and-pricing-checklist#Funeral_Pricing

9 The cost of raising a child in the United States: https://www.usda.gov/media/blog/2017/01/13/cost-raising-child

10 Similar to a level house payment in a mortgage amortization schedule, your premium payment for a life insurance policy is evenly spread out over a long period of time, even though your mortality cost increases over that same period of time.

11 Many people who purchase a ***non-guaranteed*** policy only overpay in the early years, then cancel the policy before they get to the later years.

12 Many life insurance companies have created products using the universal life design as the framework for the new product. Other design features are then added which significantly change how the policy performs. The term "traditional universal life" is used here to differentiate the original universal life design from those that have additional design features.

13 See IRS Code, Section 7702, Modified Endowment Contract. Federal law restricts how much money can be deposited into a tax-deferred cash-value life insurance policy. Mathematical formulas are used to make this determination at the time a policy is issued. Unless you plan to deposit a lot of money into a life insurance policy, this law will not impact you.

14 IRS Code, Section 1035 explained: https://www.finra.org/investors/1035-exchanges

15 Dividends come from three sources: interest, expenses and mortality. Life insurance companies set the pricing assumptions conservatively and then pay out the favorable experience in the form of dividends each year.

16 Financial gain from a ***cancelled*** life insurance policy may be taxable as income.

17 The accumulated cash value in a participating whole life policy grows tax deferred. Like any other cash-value life insurance, if the policy is ever cancelled, any financial gain may be taxable as income.

18 A funeral home will accept, as payment in full, an assignment from a life insurance policy. This arrangement can be set up with the funeral home prior to, or after death occurs. The assignment is made via a simple form, filed with the life insurance company, that allows the funeral home to be paid directly from the policy death benefit. This way, no one needs to pay for the funeral arrangements from their own pocket or credit card, nor does the decedent's other financial accounts need to be accessed to pay for the funeral.

19 www.nolhga.com - National Organization of Life & Health Insurance Guaranty Associations

About the Author

Jon Marcroft has been a career professional in the life insurance industry for more than 20 years. Currently, he is president of a multi-state independent agency, MFS Group, Inc., which works with many different life insurance companies.

He is also vice president of KINNECT, Inc., an investigations firm that operates within the financial regulatory system. Jon oversees the process of disbursements to beneficiaries and rightful heirs of unclaimed proceeds that have been reported by life insurance companies within the United States.

The life insurance industry recognized Jon for his insights into consumer demand when he was selected to serve on a panel for the Life Insurance Marketing & Research Association's (LIMRA) international distribution conference in 2008.

Jon is a strong proponent of consumer empowerment. In 2015 he founded Simplis® Life. SimplisLife.com is a secure, feature-rich, and award-winning website with custom plug-ins designed to empower consumers and simplify the life insurance purchasing experience. Go to www.SimplisLife.com to learn more.

He was born in San Diego, California, raised in Greeley, Colorado, and currently lives with his lovely wife Lucy in Salt Lake City, Utah, where they often hang out with the neighbor dogs, Bluebear and Popcorn. He is the proud parent of five adult children, and the grateful grandpa of one lively granddaughter.

Jon is left-handed.

LIMRA International

March 23, 2008

Mr. Jonathan Marcroft
Career Agent
[redacted]

Dear Jonathan;

We want to thank you for speaking at LIMRA's 2008 Distribution conference held last month in San Antonio. The feedback from the conference has been very positive.

The expertise that is presented in every session is what makes these conferences successful. I especially want to thank you for your willingness to share your insights. Your contribution has been a significant factor in the success of the conference.

We hope you will plan to attend next year's Distribution Conference February 26th and 27th at the Hilton in the Walt Disney World Resort, Lake Buena Vista, Florida.

Again, thank you for your support.

Sincerely,

Sean O'Donnell
Director, Member Relations
LIMRA

Made in the USA
Monee, IL
04 November 2026

67385880R00056